Dec 2013

Drug Cartels
and Smugglers

Drug Cartels and Smugglers

Infamous Terrorists

Mass Murderers

Modern-Day Pirates

Organized Crime

Serial Killers

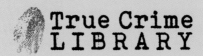
True Crime
LIBRARY

Drug Cartels and Smugglers

Carol Ellis and Robert Grayson

ELDORADO INK

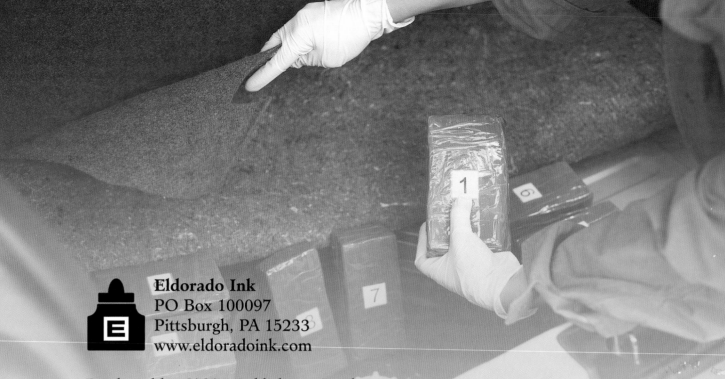

Eldorado Ink
PO Box 100097
Pittsburgh, PA 15233
www.eldoradoink.com

Produced by OTTN Publishing, Stockton, New Jersey

CPSIA compliance information: Batch#CS2013-1. For further information, contact Eldorado Ink at info@eldoradoink.com.

First printing

1 3 5 7 9 8 6 4 2

Library of Congress Cataloging-in-Publication Data
available from the Library of Congress

    ISBN-13: 978-1-61900-028-5 (hc)
    ISBN-13: 978-1-61900-029-2 (trade)
    ISBN-13: 978-1-61900-030-8 (ebook)

For information about custom editions, special sales, or premiums, please contact our special sales department at info@eldoradoink.com.

Table of Contents

A Mexican official at a border crossing examines a truck to make sure it is not carrying illegal drugs. Studies indicate that nearly 90 percent of the cocaine, marijuana, and other drugs smuggled into the United States come into the country from Mexico.

The War on Drugs
Combat with the Drug Cartels

For decades, the United States has been waging a "war on drugs." Numerous laws have made it illegal to possess, manufacture, or sell many types of dangerous, highly addictive drugs, such as cocaine, heroin, and crystal methamphetamine. Every year, Congress appropriates roughly $3 billion to the U.S. Drug Enforcement Administration (DEA), a government agency that is responsible for preventing illegal drugs from being smuggled into the United States. Other federal agencies, such as the Border Patrol, Federal Bureau of Investigation (FBI), and U.S. Coast Guard, also devote significant resources to the drug war. State and municipal governments also spend billions each year on their own efforts to break up drug rings and imprison drug dealers in their communities. In all, experts estimate that the United States spends more than $25 billion every year on anti-drug efforts.

However, these efforts have largely failed to prevent the flow of illegal drugs into the United States, or to reduce the number of Americans that use drugs. According to the annual *Monitoring the Future* survey conducted by the National Institute on Drug Abuse, in 1991 just over 29 percent of high school seniors admitted to having used an illegal drug. Twenty years later, in 2011, that figure had risen to 40 percent. A 2012 study by the National Drug Intelligence Center found that illicit drug use costs the U.S. economy more than $190 billion a year in lost worker productivity, increased health care expenses, and costs related to police activity and prison operations.

The failure of the American drug war is due in large part to the success of well-organized and well-financed drug selling operations, often referred to in the media as "drug cartels."

A *cartel* is an association of businesses that agree to work together in order to set the price for a commodity or service that they control. One well-known example of a legitimate cartel is OPEC, an international association of countries that possess significant oil reserves. OPEC affects the global price of oil by regulating the amount of oil that its members produce each year. The term *drug cartels* originated in the 1980s, when some of the major cocaine dealers in Colombia agreed to work together on production and distribution of that drug. Today, the term *drug cartels* is popularly used to refer to any criminal organization that makes its money primarily from manufacturing, smuggling and distributing illegal drugs. (In official reports the DEA, FBI, and other agencies often refer to drug cartels as "drug trafficking organizations," or DTOs.)

Today there remain several powerful Colombian drug cartels, largely because that country is the world's largest producer of cocaine. However, over the past two decades drug cartels from Mexico have come to dominate the global trade in illegal drugs. The Mexican cartels, such as the notorious Sinaloa Cartel, operate like international corporations—they make partnerships with street gangs and crime organizations in the United States and other countries in order to distribute drugs. As a result, the

DEA agents count nearly $3.5 million in U.S. currency, just a small portion of the cash and drugs seized in a 2007 drug bust that broke up a drug ring in the southwestern United States. During the operation, federal agents captured 14 tons of marijuana, 4.5 tons of cocaine, and smaller amounts of other drugs. They seized $45 million in cash along with many weapons, and arrested nearly 400 people. However, although major drug busts like this one make headlines, the truth is that they do little to weaken the power of Mexican drug cartels.

Afghan soldiers destroy poppy seeds to prevent them from being grown and processed into opium and heroin. The U.S. government spends hundreds of millions of dollars each year on programs intended to stop foreign farmers from producing plants that can be processed into illegal drugs. These include the opium poppy, grown in Afghanistan and Thailand, and coca plants, which can be processed into cocaine and are grown in the Andes Mountains of South America.

Sinaloa Cartel earns an estimated $20 billion a year in profits from its drug smuggling and selling operations.

Cartels from Central America, the Caribbean, Central Asia, Africa, China, and Russia also work in much the same way, controlling their own shares of illegal drug markets in the United States, Europe, and other places.

"[American politicians and law enforcement agencies] pretend that the cartels don't have an infrastructure in the U.S.," a former CIA officer named Fulton Armstrong told the *Washington Post* in 2012. "But you don't do a $20 billion a year business . . . with ad-hoc, part-time volunteers. You use an established infrastructure to support the markets."

FIGHTING THE WAR ON DRUGS

The enormous amounts of money that the cartels can earn makes them willing to take risks and spend money to make sure their drug shipments can get into the United States. Since the 1970s, the U.S. government has declared a "war on drugs," with many laws passed to stop the flow of drugs into the country and bring down drug dealers.

Background: Anti-Drug Legislation in the United States

The first laws meant to reduce drug use in the United States were aimed at "patent medicines," tonics promoted by shady businessmen, who claimed they could cure a variety of problems. These products, which contained ingredients like alcohol, opium, or cocaine, rarely worked. However, they were popular because they would give the user a feeling of well-being, or "high." To regulate the addictive ingredients in patent medicines, in 1906 the U.S. government passed the Pure Food and Drug Act. This legislation required patent medicine makers to list the ingredients on the label. Later amendments to the act required the manufacturers to meet standards of purity that small-town pharmacists or fly-by-night elixir salesmen could not meet.

Subsequent American laws would outlaw the sale of addictive drugs altogether. In 1914, the Harrison Narcotics Tax Act established penalties for selling opiates (a class of drugs that includes opium, heroin, and morphine) and cocaine, although the law allowed some exceptions for medical use. Further penalties were imposed by the 1922 Narcotic Drugs Import and Export Act, which made recreational use of opiates and cocaine illegal. During the 1920s, some states started banning marijuana, and a federal law making it illegal to sell marijuana was passed in 1937.

Despite the laws, people still found ways to get high. In 1924, two officials of the U.S. Public Health Service, Dr. Andrew Du Mez and Lawrence Kolb, issued a report on drug addiction in the United States. They found that about a million Americans were regularly using opiates or cocaine, and that a widespread underground traffic in illegal drugs existed in the country. The authors claimed that drugs were imported across the Canadian and Mexican borders, despite the restrictions of the Harrison Narcotics Act.

This report appeared during the Prohibition era (1920–1933), a time when the sale and manufacture of alcohol was banned in the United States. Street gangs in New York, Chicago, Detroit, Philadelphia, and other American cities had organized to take control of bootlegging, the illegal production and distribution of alcohol. Some of the gangs, notably the New York faction controlled by Charles "Lucky" Luciano, also dabbled in trafficking narcotics. The U.S. Treasury Department, which was responsible for enforcing Prohibition laws as well as the ban on narcotics, tended to focus on bootleggers, rather than drug dealers. This allowed drug dealers some freedom to operate. In 1930 the Federal Bureau of Narcotics was created to enforce anti-drug laws.

Despite this new agency, the problem of illegal drug use by Americans continued to grow over the next four decades. During the 1940s and 1950s, organized crime families became heavily involved in drug trafficking, leading to greater availability of illicit drugs in American cities. The turbulent 1960s saw a sharp increase in drug use, to the point where, by 1969, the Gallup Organization reported that 48 percent of Americans considered drug use a serious problem in their community.

In 1971, President Richard M. Nixon declared that the U.S. would wage a "war on drugs." New laws were passed intended to reduce illegal drug use, and the Drug Enforcement Administration (DEA) was created in 1973. In the 40 years since then, the U.S. government has spent over $1 trillion to stop drug trafficking. Despite this, by 2013 it seemed to many observers that powerful drug cartels were winning the war.

One important piece of legislation is the Controlled Substances Act of 1970. This law established five "schedules," or categories, of drugs and similar substances. All pharmeceuticals—from ordinary prescription drugs to dangerous narcotics—are included on one of the following schedules:

- Schedule I controlled substances are considered to have no accepted medical use while also having a high potential for abuse. Examples include ecstasy, heroin, LSD, and marijuana.
- Substances on schedule II and III can be prescribed to treat medical conditions, but they are considered to have a relatively high potential for abuse or addiction. Schedule II includes both narcotics (the painkillers morphine, codeine, and oxycodone) and stimulants (amphetamines and methamphetamine diet pills). Cocaine, which is sometimes used in certain medical procedures, is a schedule II drug.

    Schedule III includes some products that contain several different drugs, such as Tylenol with codeine, as well as anabolic steroids.
- Schedule IV and V controlled substances are drugs that have a

medicinal purpose but have a relatively low potential for abuse or addiction. Schedule IV drugs include sleep aids like Xanax, anti-anxiety drugs like Valium, and muscle relaxants like Klonopin. Schedule V drugs include some types of cough syrup that contain several controlled substances.

The Controlled Substances Act established penalties that include heavy fines and imprisonment for the illegal sale or use of drugs.

Another key law is the 1986 Anti-Drug Abuse Act, which established mandatory minimum sentences for peo-

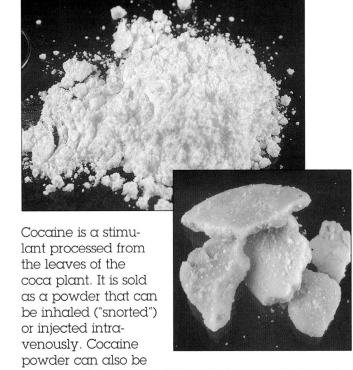

Cocaine is a stimulant processed from the leaves of the coca plant. It is sold as a powder that can be inhaled ("snorted") or injected intravenously. Cocaine powder can also be processed into a crystal-like substance called crack, which causes an intense high when smoked.

The flowers and leaves of the Cannabis plant can be dried and processed into marijuana, a drug that is smoked or eaten to produce a mild high. Hashish is a similar, but more potent, drug produced from Cannabis.

er, depending on the quantity of the drug sold and whether violence was involved. A second conviction for selling drugs includes a mandatory sentence of at least ten years, and possibly as much as a life term behind bars. (The current penalties for drug trafficking can be found in the appendix on page 83.)

Some people believe these mandatory penalties are much too harsh. Critics of the law point out that a first-time offender who sells a few hundred dollars worth of drugs faces the same penalty that the boss of a drug cartel would receive if convicted.

ple convicted of selling drugs like marijuana, crack, cocaine, heroin, meth, and PCP. Under this law, the first time a federal court convicts a person of dealing one of these drugs, the person must serve a prison sentence of at least five years. The sentence could be even high-

Since the mid-1980s, the population of U.S. prisons has risen at an alarming rate. In 1980, the U.S. had about 330,000 prison inmates—roughly 150 prison inmates for every 100,000 citizens. By 2012, the number of inmates had risen to 1.6 million, and the incarceration rate was five times higher than in 1980, at 760 inmates per 100,000

Heroin is produced from the resin of the opium poppy. It comes as a white or brown powder that can be snorted, smoked, or injected into the bloodstream with a needle. White heroin is produced in a region known as the Golden Triangle (Burma, Laos, and Thailand). Brown heroin is grown in the so-called Golden Crescent (Afghanistan, Pakistan, and Iran). Both types of the drug can be found in the United States.

citizens. Much of the increase in prison population is due to the war on drugs and the mandatory prison sentences for people convicted of drug-related offenses. Today, about 50 percent of the inmates in federal prisons and 20 percent of those in state prisons have been convicted of using or selling drugs.

Despite the huge number of arrests, they have practically no effect on the operations of drug cartels. Cartel leaders—sometimes known as "drug lords"—quickly assign new dealers and smugglers to replace those who are caught by police. Even higher-ranking officials of the cartel can be easily replaced. Unless police are able to capture the cartel's leader and destroy its infrastructure, the drugs continue to flow freely.

Another focus of the drug war has been to prevent drugs from coming into the United States. Federal agencies like the U.S. Border Patrol, U.S. Coast Guard, DEA, and FBI, among others, have been charged with preventing drug smuggling into the United States. Every year the leaders of these agencies announce numerous seizures of large drug shipments. However, as with the arrests of drug dealers, experts today

Lysergic acid diethylamide, better known as LSD, is a powerful drug that causes hallucinations. The drug is a clear liquid. It is often applied to small pieces of blotter paper, which can be held on the tongue to produce the effects.

agree that these busts hardly affect the operation, or the profits, of drug cartels.

For example, when authorities intercept a large shipment of cocaine, this should cause the street price of cocaine to rise. This is because of the economic law known as "supply and demand"—if the bust meant less of the drug was available, it could be sold for a higher price. What has actually happened, however, is that despite hundreds of

Crystal methamphetamine, also known as "ice," "crank," or "speed," is a highly addictive stimulant that can cause serious health problems in users.

Coast Guard and DEA officers pose with 86 pounds of cocaine, worth more than $1 million, which was discovered on an oil tanker off the coast of Galveston, Texas, in December 2012. Although U.S. authorities regularly interdict drug shipments, the seizures barely affect the profits of international drug cartels.

highly publicized seizures, the street price of cocaine in the United States is less than half of what it was 20 years ago. In 1992, according to DEA data, a gram of cocaine cost about $245; in 2012 that gram of coke cost about $110, with the price of a gram as low as $75 in some places. The prices of other drugs, such as marijuana and methamphetamine, are also lower now than they were two decades ago. This fact is a tes-

tament to the success that drug cartels have had getting their illegal products to users in the United States. For every shipment that is captured, many more pass over the border undetected.

Smuggling Methods

Mexico has become a key nexus of the illegal drug trade because of its location between the United States and the major drug-producing countries of

Central and South America. The FBI reports that more than 90 percent of the illegal drugs smuggled into the United States today come across the border from Mexico.

The U.S.-Mexico border is particularly vulnerable to drug smuggling because tens of thousands of people cross the border for legitimate business each day. Although Border Patrol agents attempt to carefully check every vehicle crossing from Mexico, smugglers have developed many creative hiding places in vehicles, making it extremely difficult to spot illegal drugs.

In addition, the border between the United States and Mexico stretches for nearly 2,000 miles, and passes through many remote, sparsely populated areas of desert. It is very challenging for U.S.

and Mexican authorities to patrol this long border, and drug cartels take full advantage of any potential crossing point that is overlooked. Between 2006 and 2010, the United States constructed a "border wall" to limit crossings along key stretches in Texas, Arizona, and California. However, despite the controversial security fence, Mexican traffickers continue to smuggle drugs into the United States.

Smugglers succeed in crossing the border by many creative means. For example, since the mid-1990s drug traffickers have constructed more than 90 tunnels connecting the city of Nogales, Arizona, with a city just over the border in Mexico that is also called Nogales. Some of the Nogales tunnels run for more than a half-mile underground. The

Traffickers constructed this underwater "bridge" made of sandbags to transport drugs into the United States at an unguarded spot on the U.S.-Mexico border.

A smuggling tunnel in Nogales. On the U.S. side of the border, the tunnel entrance (below) was hidden in the kitchen of a house owned by a leader of the Sinaloa drug cartel.

tunnels often feature electric lighting and ventilation systems; one tunnel even had rails and a trolley system. Tunnels opened up inside of homes or businesses on the American side of the border, where drugs could be loaded into vehicles without being spotted by the Border Patrol.

In addition to the Nogales tunnel systems, dozens of other smuggling tunnels have been found running between American and Mexican cities. In 2009, investigators discovered more than 50 tons of marijuana in a tunnel between Tijuana, Mexico, and San Diego, California.

There is no easy way to find tunnels underground. Most of the tunnels that have been discovered to date have been because of informants, often captured drug dealers who give information about

smuggling activity in exchange for a lighter sentence.

In 2011, a group of Mexican smugglers tried a unique method of going over the border fence. Using a home-made catapult, they launched small bales of marijuana across the fence to confederates in the United States. The operation was caught on a surveillance camera, but the smugglers escaped before the Border Patrol could get there.

As border defenses have been strengthened on land, drug cartels have increasingly smuggled their illicit products via sea routes to avoid detection. Drugs can be carried on commercial cargo vessels, oil tankers, and small fishing boats. They are sometimes carried on small fiberglass speedboats, which are difficult to detect on radar and fast enough to evade Coast Guard vessels.

In recent years, drug cartels have invested in submersible diesel-powered crafts known as narco-submarines. The cartels set up machine shops in the jungles of Central and South America to build the 60-foot-long crafts, at a cost of about $1 million each. That's a lot of money, considering that the narco-subs typically only make one trip, then are sunk once their cargo has been delivered. The vessels are easily worth it, however, as they can carry up to 10 tons of cocaine, valued at more than $255 million. At best, Coast Guard officials say, they are able to intercept 10 percent of the narco-subs that they observe. That doesn't include the ones that sneak through without being noticed.

Often, when authorities approach a narco-sub, the four-person crew will simply abandon the vessel and scuttle it, so that the sub sinks. The Coast Guard would pick up the stranded sailors, but would have to let them go once they reached port, because without evidence, the smugglers could not be prosecuted. This changed in 2008, when a new American law made it a crime to travel in a submersible vessel that was not registered by a national government. Now, smugglers can be sentenced to up to 20 years in prison, even if they succeed in sinking their sub.

Of course, smugglers are always trying to stay one step ahead of the authorities. A new trend is to load the drugs into a watertight submersible container that is tethered to a fishing boat. The container can't be seen because it drifts

An American patrol spotted this semi-submersible craft traveling along the Mexican coast in 2007. When American ships approached, the crew sank the vessel. The U.S. Coast Guard rescued the four crewmen, and also retrieved 11 bales of cocaine that bobbed to the surface.

Drug mules attempted to conceal bales of marijuana inside the hidden compartment on the back of this flatbed truck. They were caught at a border crossing. For every mule that is caught, however, many others pass through safely. It is impossible for border patrol agents to thoroughly search every one of the more than 120 million vehicles that pass over the U.S.-Mexico border every year.

30 feet below the surface. If a Coast Guard vessel should approach to investigate, the container can be released. It contains a directional signal, so that once the patrol is gone, the smugglers' vessel can swing back and pick up the drug shipment.

These land and sea methods can be used to bring large quantities of drugs into the country. But most drugs enter the country in much smaller quantities, carried by individual smugglers known as "drug mules." Many drug mules come into the United States on commercial flights, with drugs hidden in their luggage or under their clothing. Sometimes, the mule will hide the drugs inside their own bodies, swallowing latex balloons filled with cocaine or heroin that can be excreted once they've arrived in the U.S.

This can be very dangerous; if one of the containers bursts while inside a drug mule's stomach, that person is likely to die from the effects of ingesting such a large dose.

Some people don't even realize that they are drug mules. Drugs may be hidden in the suitcase or vehicle of an innocent person, and retrieved once the unsuspecting mule has made it across the border.

At times, drug dealers may force people to become drug mules by threatening to hurt or kill members of their family if they do not smuggle the drugs successfully. However, it is more common for the drug cartels to employ impoverished people as drug mules. Carrying drugs offers an opportunity for the person to make much more money than they could ordinarily earn. Sometimes, drug addicts agree to carry illegal substances across the border in exchange for the drugs they crave. People of both sexes and all ages have served as drug mules.

In addition to paying drug mules, the cartel leaders can ensure a successful smuggling operation by bribing customs officials and airport security screeners to ignore their drug shipments. According to federal authorities, some cartels have even worked to plant their own people in the Transportation Security Administration (TSA), the government agency that oversees airport security checks and baggage handlers. The relatively small amounts of contraband carried by drug mules that trickles through the system every day adds up to a highly profitable operation.

ALLIANCES WITH AMERICAN GANGS

Once drugs have arrived in the United States, they have to be distributed to customers. To make this happen, the major drug cartels have made alliances with street gangs in the United States. Gang members work for the cartels as smugglers and as foot soldiers, defending shipments and threatening or eliminating anyone who would interfere with the cartel's activities. In exchange, they receive the right to distribute the cartel's drugs and profit from drug sales throughout the nation.

In a 2011 report titled "National Gang Threat Assessment," the FBI reported on this trend:

> Many U.S.-based gangs have established strong working relationships with Central America and Mexico-based [drug trafficking organizations] to perpetuate the smuggling of drugs across the US-Mexico and US-Canada borders. [Mexican drug cartels] control most of the cocaine, heroin, methamphetamine, and marijuana trafficked into the United States from Mexico and regularly employ lethal force to protect their drug shipments in Mexico and while crossing the US-Mexico border. . . . They are known to regularly collaborate with U.S.-based street and prison gang members and occasionally work with select [outlaw motorcycle gangs] and White Supremacist groups, purely for financial gain.

Historically, street gangs have been formed by people with a shared racial or ethnic background, and the gangs traditionally fought bitter wars with gangs made up of people with different racial or ethnic characteristics. At one time, for example, it would have been unthinkable for a violent gang like the Aryan Brotherhood, which believes that white people are superior to all other races, to work together with Mexican drug cartels or gangs made up of Hispanics or African Americans. However, the huge profits to be made from drug dealing have led gangs to suspend their traditional ideologies in order to make money.

Street gangs in the border states like Texas, New Mexico, Arizona, and California take over distribution of drugs in Los Angeles and other western U.S. cities. They also move drugs across the country, making arrangements with gangs in the Midwest and on the East Coast to carry on the trade nationally.

THE DANGER OF DRUGS

Drugs are substances that, when ingested, affect a person's brain and central nervous system. They may change a person's mood and behavior, or affect the way that person sees or senses the world around him. Drugs like marijuana, cocaine, heroin, and crystal meth are popular because they make the user feel euphoric, or "high."

However, achieving the high can come at a cost. Drugs can be physically and psychologically addictive, meaning that a regular user's body begins to crave the drugs and it becomes nearly impossible for the person to function normally without them. Drugs can cause permanent damage to a person's heart, brain, and other organs, as well as the central nervous system, muscles, skin, and bones. Drug use can lead to many health problems, including mental illness and physical ailments. Accidental and overdose deaths among drug users are common.

Often, people become involved in selling drugs because they believe it is an easy way to make a lot of money. This can be true when you're the boss of a drug-smuggling ring. However, many economic studies indicate that low-level drug dealers don't actually make much money—often, they earn less than the minimum wage for the time they spend dealing drugs.

More importantly, drug trafficking has a devastating impact on the users and their community. The rate of murder among drug dealers is considerably higher than in the regular population. A person who becomes involved in drug trafficking is highly likely to wind up in one of two places: prison or a cemetery.

DEA agents arrest Juan Carlos Ramirez-Abadia, a notorious Colombian drug smuggler, in August 2007.

Silver or Lead

Pablo Escobar and the Medellín Cartel

In May 1976, Pablo Escobar Gaviria was returning to his home in Medellín, Colombia, when he was arrested by local police. Several of Escobar's associates were also arrested. The police claimed that the men had 39 pounds (18 kg) of cocaine in their possession. However, after Escobar bribed a local judge, the case was dropped.

This was an early example of Escobar's policy of *plata o plomo* ("silver or lead")—that is, take a bribe or take a bullet. Throughout his life as one of the world's most ruthless drug lords, Escobar lived by that tenet. Bribing or killing made little difference, so long as no one interfered in his illegal business. During his reign of narco-terrorism, Escobar was linked to the deaths of more than 600 police officers, who were gunned down by his cartel's hit men.

One pilot who worked for the drug kingpin said of Escobar, "He was a gang-

ster, pure and simple. Everybody, right from the start, was afraid of him. Even later, when they considered themselves friends, everybody was afraid of him."

Cocaine provided Escobar with the riches he always dreamed of and he was not about to let anyone get in his way. He ran an operation, the Medellín Cartel, that at its height was smuggling 15 tons of cocaine, with a street value of $500 million, into the United States every day. Escobar used warehouses to store his illegal cash—there was too much of it to deposit in banks without raising suspicion.

Born into poverty in 1949, Pablo Emilio Escobar Gaviria was the third of seven children. His mother was an elementary school teacher and his father a farmer in Rionegro, Antioguia, Colombia. The family moved to Medellín when young Pablo was only two years old.

Escobar began his criminal career as a teenager, learning from other young street criminals. He was said to have started out by stealing gravestones, sanding off the names, and reselling them. He soon moved up to stealing cars. Escobar also dabbled in everything from producing fake lottery tickets to selling contraband to kidnapping for ransom. Escobar made money on these illicit deals, and became involved in

Medellín, Colombia's second-largest city, is located in the Andes Mountains, one of the few places in the world where coca plants can grow. Proximity to the cocaine source, coupled with Medellín's large airport, made the city an attractive hub for drug smugglers during the 1970s and 1980s.

drug trafficking almost by accident. Selling stolen items simply grew too competitive and dangerous, so Escobar started looking for a new racket.

During the mid-1970s, there were no drug cartels in Colombia. The drug trade was run by a handful of people. These were not seasoned tough guys; they were upscale social climbers who profited by bringing drugs to fashionable parties. These men were not in a position to exploit Colombia's full potential in the cocaine market. At most, these small-time drug dealers would put together one or two large shipments of cocaine to the United States a year.

Escobar recognized that American demand for the white powder was much greater than the current supply. He believed the time was right to build a cocaine empire, and it had to be ruled by a man with an iron fist. Using some of the money he had made in his previous criminal ventures, and incorporating the gang he had assembled through the years, in 1975 Escobar decided to muscle his way into the cocaine trade. He purchased a small airplane and began smuggling cocaine into the United States. He also arranged the murder of Fabio Restrepo, a local Medellín drug chief. When Restrepo was found dead, Escobar took over his organization and declared himself the new cocaine chief in Medellín.

Restrepo was not the only drug dealer in Medellín. Others with profitable drug businesses included Carlos Lehder, Jose Rodriguez Gacha, and the Ochoa brothers. Although Escobar had more men than these drug dealers, if they battled for control of the market all of their businesses would have suffered. Escobar had another idea—he wanted everyone to work together and create a cartel in Medellín so powerful that no law enforcement or government agency could ever shut it down. At Escobar's urging, the Medellín drug dealers all pooled their resources and developed a cartel with enough influence and money to bribe the police, the military, and the government. Airport officials and bankers were also in the cartel's pocket. Those who did not go along with what the cartel wanted were killed: no investigations were ever conducted, no arrests were ever made. Yet it was quite clear who was responsible for the murders.

The Medellín cartel operated its illegal cocaine business in a systematic, organized manner that mirrored the way the world's biggest and most successful corporations were run. Escobar was in charge of the operation. The other drug dealers did not complain because everyone made so much money. Staggering amounts of cash came to Medellín by the planeload. The Medellín cartel had 10 accountants to keep track of the drug ring's transac-

Case File

Pablo Escobar Gaviria

Born: *December 1, 1949*

Known for: *created and ran the Medellín Cartel, the largest and most violent drug cartel of the 1980s and early 1990s. Indicted on charges of drug smuggling (primarily cocaine), murder, money laundering, and political corruption*

Died: *December 2, 1993, while trying to escape from police*

tions, making sure no one along the way was skimming off the top. If any of the cartel's employees did get greedy, they were killed; oftentimes their family members were murdered as well, as a warning to others not to try to cheat Pablo Escobar.

Escobar used some of his money to buy loyalty. He would distribute money to the poor in Medellín by building housing, churches, soccer fields, and schools. He also gave out food to the disadvantaged. He cast himself as a modern-day Robin Hood. As a result, the townspeople would serve as lookouts for him, hide evidence from local authorities, and do whatever it took to protect Escobar and his empire.

Pablo Escobar in 1988.

In 1982, U.S. President Ronald Reagan created a cabinet-level task force to crack down on drug smuggling. Vice President George H. W. Bush, a former director of the CIA, headed the effort. Not only did Bush focus on stopping drugs from entering the United States, but he urged the force to go after the drug lords themselves. That put Pablo Escobar in the crosshairs. Catching the crime boss, however, remained a difficult task, especially without any substantive help from Colombian officials. Although lower-echelon members of Escobar's operation were apprehended, it took years before anyone in the top ranks was taken into custody, even with U.S. pressure being brought on the Colombian government.

Though few Colombians were willing to stand up to Escobar, a political reformer by the name of Luis Carlos Galán could not be bought or intimidated by him. Galán wanted to rid Colombia of its drug kingpins. He lost a close election for president in 1982 to Belisario Betancur, who was not willing to crack down on Colombia's drug business. But Galán was determined to destroy the drug lords and bring respectability back to his country, as well as to restore Colombia's image abroad. While none of Colombia's cocaine traffickers escaped Galán's wrath, he singled out Escobar, blaming

By the early 1980s, Colombia was known as the cocaine capital of the world. That made it a target of the United States, which was trying to stop smugglers from bringing drugs into the country. The Medellín Cartel was responsible for smuggling 80 percent of the cocaine distributed in the U.S. Colombian government officials— whether paid off or just scared—were not anxious to do anything to stop the illegal drug trade. But U.S. law enforcement officials were.

him for the ruthless bloodletting that gripped Medellín because of the drug kingpin's vast criminal empire.

After he sat out the 1986 election, Galán declared in July 1989 that he would be a candidate for president in 1990. The timing was right for the charismatic, hard-driving Galán, who was riding a wave of popularity in a country growing tired of the violence associated with the drug trade. Galán pledged to make wholesale arrests of drug dealers and extradite those who were wanted by the United States, something the U.S. government had been demanding for years.

Escobar feared that if Galán won election he would wind up in a U.S. prison. In 1984 the drug lord had been indicted for drug trafficking by a U.S. grand jury in Miami, along with other cartel leaders like Carlos Lehder, Jorge Ochoa, and Jose Rodriguez Gacha. To protect the Medellín Cartel, Escobar decided that Galán needed to die. At a rally on August 18, 1989, in Soacha, Colombia, just southwest of Bogotá, Galán was gunned down by Escobar's hit men.

The assassination of Luis Carlos Galán did not free Escobar to continue his business unimpeded. Instead, it turned many Colombians against him. Escobar soon became public enemy num-

Luis Carlos Galán

ber one in the country.

Now he was a hunted man. César Gaviria, one of Galán's allies, carried the torch for his fallen friend and won the presidency in 1990. Gaviria immediately created a special team of highly trained Colombian national police officers, known as Search Bloc, to track down Escobar and bring him to justice. In raid after raid, Search Bloc started taking down Escobar's close associates, including relatives who were in business with him. The drug boss remained on the run, however.

In an attempt to get the government to negotiate a surrender deal with him, Escobar masterminded a series of high-profile kidnappings in mid-1990. The plan worked, and in June 1991 the crime boss gave himself up on his own terms, which included no extradition to the United States. He was incarcerated in La Catedral, a prison the government allowed Escobar to build for himself, which featured luxurious accommodations and lax supervision.

The United States called the imprisonment a charade. Escobar continued to run his crime operation from prison. Under pressure to do something, the Colombian government decided to move Escobar to a real prison on July 22, 1992. But he got wind of

The body of Pablo Escobar lies on a Medellín rooftop after the notorious cartel leader was gunned down by Colombian police, December 2, 1993.

the plan and escaped from La Catedral. Once again Search Bloc went after Escobar—this time with the help of the United States, including the army's elite special ops unit Delta Force.

For a year and a half, the crime boss remained one step ahead of his pursuers, going from hiding place to hiding place. But on December 2, 1993, Search Bloc traced a call Escobar was making from a group of row houses in a poor section of Medellín. When they went into one of the homes, Escobar and a bodyguard jumped out a window onto the roof of a neighboring house. As gunfire raged, a rooftop-to-rooftop pursuit ensued. Finally, after a few minutes, Pablo Escobar, Colombia's most feared criminal, was shot dead at the age of 44.

Cali Cartel

Businessmen of Drug Trafficking

During the 1960s and early 1970s, the most popular drugs among young people were marijuana and LSD, while hardcore addicts injected heroin. By the late 1970s, however, the drug habits of Americans began to change. Almost overnight, it seemed, use of cocaine became glamorous and chic, with movie stars, rock stars, athletes, and other celebrities very open about their use of the drug.

Of course, there was a dark story behind the cocaine that found its way into the glittering urban disco scene of the late 1970s. Ruthless drug lords had turned the South American nation of Colombia into a narco-state—a country that is controlled and corrupted by drug dealers. The climate in Colombia is ideal for growing the coca plant, which can be processed into cocaine. As the drug's popularity grew during the 1970s, drug cartels formed in Colombian cities.

Their leaders supervised the cocaine trade, from cultivation of the coca crop in remote jungles to the refinement, packaging, shipment, and delivery of the drug to street dealers in the United States. Drug kingpins such as Jose Rodriguez Gacha, Pablo Escobar, and the Ochoa brothers made billions of dollars, controlled politicians, financed private security forces, and, essentially established their own laws.

While Escobar's Medellín Cartel was the most infamous of the Colombian drug cartels, throughout its heyday it had a serious rival for control of the cocaine trade—the Cali Cartel. Based in the Colombian city of Cali, this organization was formed in the 1970s by two brothers, Gilberto and Miguel Rodriguez Orejeula, and their friend José Santacruz Londoño. The men started out smuggling marijuana, but soon switched to cocaine because of the

Case File

Gilberto Rodriguez Orejeula

Born: *January 30, 1939*

Known for: *leader of the Cali Cartel, which by the mid-1990s controlled some 90 percent of the cocaine traffic in the United States. Arrested in Colombia in 1995 and extradited to the U.S. in 2004 to face charges of drug trafficking and money laundering*

Outcome: *Currently serving 30-year sentence in an American prison*

higher profits they could earn from selling the white powder.

The Cali Cartel was organized differently than the Medellín Cartel. Instead of an overall leader who was involved in every aspect of the cartel's operation, like Escobar, Cali consisted of a group of independent cells, each of which operated its own small cocaine processing and distributing business. Members of a cell reported to a cell manager, who in turn reported back to the cartel leaders. This way, even if a cell was infiltrated or busted by police, the cartel's leaders were in no danger. They could soon put a new cell in place to take over the busted cell's operations.

At the top level, the cartel was divided into five groups. Each one was responsible for a particular activity. One group was in charge of moving the cocaine (trafficking). Another made sure shipments were protected and when necessary acted as enforcers keeping drug dealers and cell managers in line. Another group was involved in Colombian politics, making connections with local and national government representatives. A financial group took care of laundering the cartel's illegal earnings, to make them appear legitimate. Finally, the legal group represented the cartel and its members in court when necessary.

The Cali Cartel differed from Escobar's Medellín Cartel in other respects as well. It was not as violent or ruthless as the Medellín group, preferring bribery over intimidation. Where the Medellín group essentially waged a war against the Colombian government during the 1980s, the Cali Cartel kept a lower profile. The organization provided cash and favors to Colombian politicians, who in turn agreed not to interfere with its drug trafficking activities. "According to the philosophy of the Cali Cartel, it is preferable to bribe than to kill," a Colombian investigative reporter told the *Los Angeles Times* in 1989.

That's not to say that the Cali Cartel did not use violence when necessary. As people moved up in the organization, it was understood that if they talked to police, their families would be tortured or killed. Cartel members who lost shipments or made mistakes were often killed as well. But the cartel was not as indiscriminate in its violence as Escobar's Medellín group. Because of this, the cartel gained a reputation as a moderate, business-like organization and its leaders became known as the "gentlemen of Cali."

Gilberto Rodriguez Orejeula was the brains behind the Cali Cartel, responsible for overall strategy and long-term planning. His brother Miguel was in charge of the cartel's daily operations. José Santacruz Londoño oversaw smuggling of drugs between Colombia and New York, where he had connections, and made sure that the cash from drug deals made its way back to Cali.

As the cartel's operations grew, vast sums of cash were shipped to Cali. The cartel leaders invested these funds into legitimate Colombian businesses. The Rodriguez Orejeula brothers opened a national chain of discount drugstores, a radio network, and a bus line in Cali. They purchased one of Colombia's top professional soccer teams, America de Cali. José Santacruz Londoño bought a taxi company in Bogotá. All three men purchased large ranches and other real estate throughout Colombia.

Thanks to his business empire, during the early 1980s Gilberto Rodriguez Orejeula was appointed chairman of the board of a Colombian bank, Banco de Trabajadores. He was able to use this bank to launder funds for the Cali Cartel. Gilberto would later start another financial institution, the First Interamericas Bank. Based in Panama, First Interamericas took advantage of the country's lax banking regulations to

These packages of cocaine are labeled with a scorpion, indicating that they belonged to Henry Loaiza-Ceballos. Nicknamed El Alacran ("the Scorpion"), Loaiza-Ceballos was a Colombian drug dealer who managed one of the Cali Cartel cells.

Gilberto Rodriguez Orejuela (left) was the master-mind of the Cali Cartel. He was known as "the Chess Player" because of his strategic planning. His brother Miguel (right) oversaw the cartel's day-to-day operations.

launder money for both the Cali and Medellín cartels during the late 1980s, a time when Manuel Noriega controlled Panama.

The Cali Cartel was innovative, finding creative ways to ship drugs into the United States. The cartel built secret airstrips and hidden warehouses to hide their drugs. They worked with Mexican drug lords to ship cocaine by land over the U.S. border, and smuggled drugs by ship into southern Florida. When the demand for cocaine began to drop in the United States during the late 1980s, the cartel opened new markets for the drug in Europe. The cartel also took the step of expanding its cocaine production outside of Colombia, setting up operations in Bolivia and Peru. Like Colombia, these Andean countries had the right combination of climate and altitude to grow coca plants properly.

For most of its history, the Cali Cartel kept a low profile. Its leaders were happy to rake in enormous profits without notoriety. But when Colombian police began pressuring Pablo Escobar because of his attacks on government figures, Cali leaders saw an opportunity to increase their share of the cocaine trade. During the late 1980s and early 1990s, the two cartels fought for control of drugs and smuggling routes. Cali even made several attempts to kill Escobar, but none succeeded.

Despite this, the Cali organization continued to grow, in large part because Colombian police mostly left them alone while focused on bringing down the Medellín Cartel. Soon after Escobar was killed in 1993, the Cali Cartel was believed to control 80 percent of the international cocaine trade, as well as 30 percent of global heroin trafficking. The cartel's profits were estimated at $7 billion a year.

But the war between the cartels had eroded the public view of Cali as less violent. Soldiers of the cartel had been involved in bombings and had murdered rival drug smugglers and others. Perhaps the worst abuses had occurred in the town of Trujillo, near Cali, where members of the cartel had killed nearly 350 people between 1988 and 1994. Some of the murders had been committed to warn people not to cross the Cali Cartel; other people were killed because

The Cali Cartel bribed hundreds of Colombian politicians during its time in power. In the mid-1990s, evidence surfaced showing that Cali had donated significant amounts of money to the election campaign of Ernesto Sampler, who served as Colombia's president from 1994 to 1998. As president, Sampler refused to turn Cali Cartel leaders over to U.S. authorities for trial in Miami on drug trafficking and money laundering charges. Other Cali-bribed congressmen made sure that Sampler remained in office despite the election funding scandal.

they supported certain factions in the country's civil war, or were simply considered undesirable, such as thieves or prostitutes. One person killed was the local Roman Catholic priest, Father Tiberio Fernández, who was tortured and executed, his body dumped into the Cauca River. The local Colombian police knew the cartel was committing these atrocities but took no action; a Colombian military unit in the area actually assisted in some of the killings.

In addition to pressure from the Colombian public, the United States was becoming more involved in efforts to disrupt the cocaine trade. The Colombian government agreed to work with American DEA agents, and soon the special police force known as Search Bloc would turn its attention to the Cali Cartel.

During the summer of 1995, the cartel's top leaders were arrested. Perhaps remembering what had happened to Escobar, Gilberto Rodriguez Orejuela told police, "Easy boys. Don't kill me. I am a man of peace," when he was discovered hiding at an apartment he owned in

Cali in June 1995. José Santacruz Londoño was arrested in July, and Miguel Rodriguez Orejeula was caught in August. Colombian police also arrested most of the cell managers—including Henry "El Alacran" Loaiza-Ceballos—and hundreds of low-level cartel members.

The arrests effectively destroyed the Cali Cartel. It turned out that a former high-ranking member of the organization named Jorge Salcedo had decided to work with the DEA and Colombian authorities to bring down the cartel. Salcedo was a former Colombian military officer who had been hired to kill Pablo Escobar in 1989. Although his attempt failed, the Rodriguez Orejeula brothers liked him and placed Salcedo in charge of their security operations. By early 1995 Salcedo was disillusioned with the cartel and agreed to become an informant for the DEA.

Although all of the Cali Cartel's top leaders had been indicted in the United

States on drug trafficking charges, the Colombian government refused to extradite them. (During the late 1980s, drug traffickers had bribed Colombian officials to rewrite the country's constitution, making extradition illegal.) José Santacruz Londoño escaped briefly from a Colombian prison, but was killed by police in 1996.

The Rodriguez Orejeula brothers remained in a Colombian prison, from which they continued to direct the remnants of their cartel. Other small groups also formed in Colombia to fill the void left by the fall of the Cali and Medellín cartels. These smaller groups tended to specialize in one particular area of drug trafficking. Some groups were involved in cultivating coca and processing it into cocaine; others specialized in transporting the drug; others set up distribution networks. These organization made deals with Mexican drug lords, who took over the task of smuggling cocaine

The Rodriguez Orejeula brothers used their Drogas la Rebaja chain of discount drugstores to launder money from their drug smuggling operations. The Colombian chain was highly successful—it was valued at $216 billion and operated more than 400 stores in 28 cities throughout the country. In 2004, the government seized control of Drogas la Rebaja because it had been funded with money from illegal cartel activities.

After being elected president of Colombia in 2002, Álvaro Uribe cooperated with American officials in their "war on drugs." He arranged for the Rodriguez Orejeula brothers to be extradited to the U.S.

into the United States and other countries. The decline of the Colombian cartels thus led to the rise of the powerful Mexican cartels that dominate the cocaine trade today.

In 2002, a Colombian judge released Gilberto Rodriguez Orejuela from prison on parole for good behavior. This move provoked outrage in Colombia, and he was soon re-arrested on new drug trafficking charges. Two years later, Colombia's government agreed to extradite Gilberto to the United States to face trial on drug trafficking and money laundering charges. Miguel was extradited to the U.S. in 2005.

In September 2006, the Rodriguez Orejuela brothers pled guilty to drug charges in Miami. They agreed to forfeit $2.1 billion in assets, and were each sentenced to 30 years in prison. "These guilty pleas deal a final and fatal blow to the Cali Cartel, a violent drug trafficking organization that once operated outside of the law," U.S. Attorney General Alberto Gonzales said at their sentencing. "But as drug traffickers and kingpins around the world now know, they are not beyond the reach of justice in the United States—the Cali Cartel has been dismantled and the brothers now face years in American prisons. Their arrests, extradition to the United States and now their convictions were all made possible by extraordinary cooperation from the Colombian government, our valued partner in the fight to eradicate narcotics trafficking and the violence that so often accompanies it."

American soldiers parachute into Panama during Operation Just Cause, a 1989 military operation to capture the country's military leader, Manuel Noriega. During the 1980s Noriega allowed Panama to become a center for drug smuggling and money laundering.

Manuel Noriega

Narco-State Kingpin

On December 20th, 1989, U.S. President George H. W. Bush gave the order for more than 13,000 American soldiers to invade the Central American nation of Panama. They joined some 12,000 U.S. troops already stationed in Panama, and became part of the largest U. S. military action since the Vietnam War. The purpose of their invasion: to arrest a drug lord who was using Panama as a base of operations.

It is not unusual for the United States and other powerful countries to go after drug lords. After all, these criminals spread misery and violence, cause instability, and ally themselves with terrorists and rogue states in ways that can endanger entire regions. However, the drug lord captured by U.S. troops in 1989 was quite unusual. His name was General Manuel Noriega, and he had ruled Panama for six years. Noriega, the

former head of Panama's armed forces, was also a man that U.S. leaders had once considered a valuable ally in the region.

Manuel Antonio "Tony" Noriega Moreno was born on February 11, 1934, in Terraplén, a poor section of Panama City. Orphaned by the time he was five, Tony was raised by relatives and grew up in a run-down area of the city, which is the capital of Panama.

As a teenager, Noriega attended high school at the Instituto Nacional. He wanted to continue his education and study medicine, but his family didn't have nearly enough money to send him to medical school. Instead, Noriega enrolled in the Chorillos Military Academy in Peru. A relative who worked at the Panamanian embassy was able to help Noriega get a scholarship to the facility. At the time, the military offered the most options for poor young men. Noriega would soon take advantage of those options.

While Noriega was studying at Chorillos from 1958 to 1962, he was contacted by an agent with the U.S. Central Intelligence Agency (CIA). At this time, the United States and Soviet Union were engaged in the Cold War. In Latin American countries, the CIA often put out feelers to young members of the military, hoping that one day, when they had high-ranking positions, they would support American interests in the Cold War. At this initial contact, Noreiga agreed to provide information about fellow cadets—particularly those who were sympathetic to the Soviet Union—for a fee. This marked the start of Noriega's long relationship with U.S. intelligence agencies.

Despite his humble background, Noriega excelled in military school. After he graduated in 1962, he worked as a surveyor in the Panama Canal Zone, then joined Panama's army, the National Guard, as a member of the staff of Major Omar Torrijos.

Noriega became a favorite of Torrijos, and quickly moved into powerful positions in the military. Because he

Cargo ships enter the locks at the Atlantic entrance to the Panama Canal. The Canal was of vital strategic importance to the United States, because American warships could use it to pass relatively quickly from the Atlantic to the Pacific oceans in the event of a crisis.

also continued providing information to the CIA, he was invited to receive additional training from the U.S. military. In 1967 he studied at the School of the Americas, a U.S. Army training facility for Latin American cadets and officers in Panama. He also took a course in psychological warfare at the U.S. Army base at Fort Bragg, North Carolina. This training helped Noriega continue to rise through the ranks.

In 1968, Noriega's mentor Torrijos took part in a coup d'etat that overthrew the elected president, Arnulfo Arias. The Panamanian military seized power, and by 1969 Torrijos had emerged as the country's de facto ruler. Noreiga had assisted in the coup against Arias, and supported Torrijos in the struggle for power among the military leaders. He was rewarded with a promotion to major and control of a large number of Panamanian troops.

The position enabled Noriega to profit from illegal activities that occurred in the military district he controlled. He received bribes in exchange for ignoring criminal activities and for helping to rig local elections so that certain candidates would win.

In 1970 Noriega received another promotion, to lieutenant colonel, and was placed in charge of Panama's military intelligence bureau. In this position Noriega could gather information on Panamanians. He used it to blackmail

Case File

Manuel Noriega Moreno

Born: *February 11, 1934*

Known for: *as military leader of Panama from 1983 to 1989, allowed drug traffickers to use the country as a base of operations. In 1989 the U.S. military arrested Noriega and brought him to the United States to face trial*

Outcome: *in prison since 1989, Noriega is currently serving a 20-year sentence in Panama*

people into doing what he wanted. He also became involved with a group that smuggled heroin into the United States. Noriega used his official position to protect the people who actually did the smuggling, including his mentor's older brother, Moisés Torrijos.

Some members of the U.S. government were concerned about Noriega's involvement in the drug trade. As early as 1971, the DEA wanted to indict the Panamanian spy chief for drug trafficking. However, Noriega was still working with the CIA, and the agency persuaded American authorities not to follow up on the charges. Ironically, Omar Torrijos would later name Noriega to be the country's official liaison with the

U.S. President Jimmy Carter poses with General Omar Torrijos at a 1978 ceremony for the ratification of the Panama Canal treaties

DEA, making him the person in charge of all drug-trafficking investigations in Panama.

During the mid-1970s, the Torrijos government began negotiating with the United States over control of the Panama Canal Zone. When the United States had decided to build a canal across the isthmus of Panama in 1903, the government had signed a treaty with the newly formed nation of Panama that gave the U.S. permanent control of the canal, along with a strip of territory roughly five miles wide on either side.

This area, known as the Canal Zone, was governed by U.S., not Panamanian, laws and had its own police force and judges. Essentially, it was a 550-square-mile piece of American territory in the middle of a foreign country. Over the years, Panamanians came to resent the existence of the Canal Zone.

In September 1977 U.S. President Jimmy Carter and Panama's Torrijos signed treaties in which the United States agreed to turn control of the Canal Zone over to Panama. The Zone handover would be gradual, with Panama taking full control in 1999. However, because of the Panama Canal's strategic importance to the U.S. Navy, a provision of the treaty allowed U.S. forces to intervene in Panama to defend the Canal if necessary.

As part of the Canal treaty negotiations, General Torrijos had promised to end military rule over Panama. He said that he would step down and allow a civilian election in 1984. Before this could happen, however, Torrijos died in a plane crash in 1981.

Over the next two years, military leaders fought for control of Panama. Noriega eventually outmaneuvered his rivals, and by 1983 had taken control of Panama's military. Even though Panama had a president and a legislature, they held little actual power. The military was the institution that actually ran the country. As leader of the army, Noriega became de facto ruler of Panama.

To American leaders, this was not an unwelcome development at first. Torrijos had been suspected of sympathizing with the Soviet Union; Noriega was believed to be a staunch supporter of the United States. Noriega supported the U.S.-backed government in El Salvador, which was fighting against Soviet-backed rebels. He also helped the U.S. government secretly funnel money to rebel groups in Nicaragua that were fighting the Soviet-supported Sandinista government.

Soon, though, Noriega went from being a valuable asset to a big problem for the U.S. For one thing, his rule in Panama was brutal and cruel. The police and soldiers attacked and arrested anyone who dared to dissent against his rule. In 1985, Hugo Spadafora, a well-known physician who spoke out

against Noriega's rule, was found dead. Noriega claimed that he had nothing to do with the murder, but few people believed him. Years later, a Panamanian court convicted Noriega in absentia of conspiracy in the killing.

The CIA also began to suspect that Noriega was playing both sides in the intelligence game—taking money from the U.S. for information about Communist activities in Cuba and Latin America, while at the same time getting paid by Cuba for information about American activities in the region.

Another problem was his continued involvement in drug trafficking. By the late 1970s, Noriega had started to become involved with the infamous Medellín Cartel. This Colombian organization made astonishing profits smuggling cocaine into the United States and other countries. Noriega helped the car-

One of Noriega's "dignity battalions"—paramilitary groups that he used to terrorize anyone who opposed his control—marches through the streets of Panama City, 1989.

DEA agents escort Noriega onto a U.S. Air Force aircraft that will take him back to the United States for his trial on drug charges, January 1990.

tel by laundering its money, providing the cartel with crucial cover for its crimes. In return, the cartel paid Noriega millions of dollars. The Panamanian strongman also continued to run his own drug smuggling operations. By the late 1980s, Noriega was solidly in control of the drug trade in Panama. He had made himself a multimillionaire thanks to drug money, but he had badly damaged his relationship with the United States.

In February 1988, after a 14-month investigation, the U.S. Department of Justice issued two indictments that charged Noriega with drug trafficking. Noriega denied the charges and refused to go to the United States for a court hearing. As long as he remained in Panama, Noriega was beyond the reach of U.S. law. Preparations were secretly made to invade Panama and oust Noriega.

During the run-up to a presidential election in 1989, Noriega's supporters formed paramilitary gangs called "dignity battalions," which roved the streets threatening and intimidating Noriega's opponents. Despite this, during the May 1989 election, Noriega's candidate for president, Carlos Duque, lost the popular vote by a wide margin. The general immediately released false voting results and claimed victory. A few days later, the politicians who had opposed Noriega's man, Guillermo Endara and Guillermo Ford, were attacked and brutally beaten on the streets of Panama City by members of one of the dignity battalions. The stolen election, and the behavior of Noriega's thugs, roused international anger against the regime.

In 1989, when a U.S. Marine stationed in the Canal Zone was killed during an altercation with Panamanian troops, President Bush gave the order to send in the troops. The invasion of Panama, which began on December 20, 1989, was code-named Operation Just Cause.

Faced with the overwhelming American invasion force, Panamanian troops quickly surrendered. Noriega fled to the Vatican embassy in Panama City. Embassies are considered sovereign territory, so the U.S. forces could not enter and remove the wanted drug lord. Instead, U.S. forces surrounded the embassy and set up loudspeakers. They played loud music and broadcast messages telling Noriega to surrender.

The standoff lasted for 10 days. Finally, Noriega couldn't stand it anymore. On January 3, 1990, he left the embassy and surrendered to U.S. forces. Noriega was arrested and flown to Miami, where he was charged with drug trafficking and money laundering.

There was plenty of evidence against Noriega, but his trial was somewhat embarrassing for the U.S. government. Noriega was more than happy to share the history of his long collaboration with the CIA. Although the court declared some of the details irrelevant to the trial, the CIA was forced to admit that it had given money to Noriega for his services. Noriega claimed he had received $10 million, while the U.S. government insisted he had been paid only $320,000. The exact amount was never determined. Ultimately, it didn't matter. Noriega was convicted on eight counts and sentenced to 30 years in prison.

Noriega's sentence was later reduced to 17 years, and he was released from U.S. custody in 2007. However, he was then turned over to France, which wanted to place him on trial for laundering money used by the Medellín Cartel to purchase French property. In 2010, Noriega was tried and convicted in France, and was sentenced to seven years in prison.

In 2011, however, the French government released Noriega to Panamanian authorities. He was taken to Panama, where he had been convicted in absentia on charges of corruption and murder dating from his years in power. Noriega remains in a Panamanian prison.

Guerra Contra el Narco
The History of Mexico's Violent Drug War

Since the mid-2000s, Mexico has been torn by a violent conflict between Mexican drug cartels and the government. The violence is worst in the Mexican states that border the United States, as these are where drug smugglers are concentrated. Since 2004, more than 60,000 people, many of them low-level drug couriers, cartel soldiers, or Mexican civilians, have died. Mexican federal police have arrested more than 120,000 people connected with drug cartels. Despite government pressure, and more than $1 billion in support from the United States, the conflict shows little sign of easing any time soon.

Most of the Mexican drug cartels that are fighting against the government today originated during the early 1980s. They were smuggling organizations hired by the Colombian cartels to bring their drugs over the border into the United States. Eventually, these groups took over a larger share of drug production and distribution. Today, it is estimated that Mexican cartels control about 90 percent of the illegal drugs that are smuggled into the U.S.

The long U.S.-Mexico border has long been vulnerable to smugglers. For example, during the Prohibition era (1920–1933), bootleggers brought alcohol into the United States from Mexico.

As the demand for illegal drugs like marijuana and heroin grew during the 1960s, Mexican gangs began to sneak large amounts of these substances over the border. Both cannabis plants and opium poppies have been grown in Mexico for generations, so it was convenient for smugglers to traffick those drugs.

The coca plants from which cocaine is produced do not naturally grow in Mexico, however, so Mexican smugglers rarely moved cocaine on a large scale until the early 1980s. Cocaine was the province of the Colombian cartels. Their preferred smuggling routes took the drugs from Colombia to islands in the Caribbean, then into southern Florida. As U.S. law enforcement shut down these routes, drug lords like Pablo Escobar began looking for other ways to get their product into the United States. Escobar made arrangements with Mexican marijuana and heroin traffickers, and they were soon carrying Colombian cocaine over the border.

One of the first major drug trafficking organizations in Mexico was the Guadalajara Cartel. It was formed by Miguel Ángel Félix Gallardo, a former member of Mexico's federal police. Félix Gallardo used his connections with police and local politicians to protect his smuggling operations. The Guadalajara Cartel initially dealt in marijuana and heroin, but in the early 1980s Félix Gallardo began smuggling cocaine for Pablo Escobar, using his established routes.

At first, Escobar paid for Félix Gallardo's smuggling services in cash, but the groups soon worked out an arrangement by which the Mexicans would receive a share of every cocaine shipment—usually 35 to 50 percent of the drugs—to sell for themselves. During the 1980s traffickers could earn much more money from selling cocaine than they could from selling marijuana or other drugs. The connection with Medellín made Félix Gallardo the most powerful drug lord in Mexico, as denoted by his nickname El Padrino ("The Godfather").

Félix Gallardo was cunning and ruthless. When one of his secret marijuana farms was raided by federal police in

U.S. Border Patrol agents found these bales of marijuana when they stopped a smugglers' boat off the coast of California in 2012. The 6,600 pounds of marijuana had a street value of nearly $10 million. Because marijuana grows well in Mexico, the drug has been smuggled into the United States in large quantites since the late 1960s.

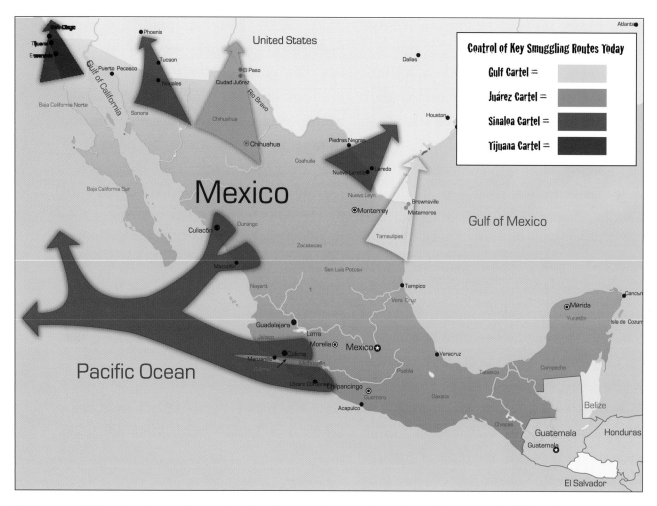

This map of Mexico shows the major border crossing routes where drugs are trafficked.

1984, he had the man who had told the Mexican authorities kidnapped, tortured, and murdered in early 1985. The victim, Enrique Camarena, had been an undercover operative for the DEA, and the American agency intensified its investigation of the Guadalajara Cartel. Two of the cartel's top figures, Ernesto Fonseca Carrillo and Rafael Caro Quintero, were arrested in 1985, but Félix Gallardo was able to use his political connections to stay out of prison.

With the pressure continuing, Félix Gallardo decided to divide responsibility for his drug trafficking routes among several smaller gangs. This way, even if police busted one gang, the others could continue their smuggling operations. All of the gangs would pay Félix Gallardo for the right to those territories, and he would continue to use his government contacts to protect their smuggling operations. However, Félix Gallardo would no longer control the day-to-day operations on the different drug routes; those would become the responsibility of each gang. Félix Gallardo put his plan into action in 1987, after meeting with key associates at a resort in Acapulco.

Under Félix Gallardo's new arrangement, seven of his nephews, the Arellano Félix brothers, would control the drug routes in the Mexican state of Baja California. Their turf would include all smuggling from Tijuana, Mexico, into San Diego, California, the most heavily populated crossing spot along the U.S.-Mexico border. The Arellano Félix organization would become known as the Tijuana Cartel.

Control over drugs in Ciudad Juárez, a city on the Rio Grande, would go to Rafael Aguilar Guajardo, an associate of Félix Gallardo who operated in that area. Ciudad Juárez and the American city on the other side of the Rio Grande, El Paso, Texas, make up the second most populous cross-border location. Félix Gallardo assigned brothers Amado and Vicente Carrillo Fuentes, the nephews of his imprisoned lieutenant Ernesto Fonseca Carrillo, to assist with Guajardo's operation, which became known as the Juárez Cartel.

Drug distribution from Sonora, a Mexican state that borders Arizona and New Mexico, was given to an organization run by Miguel Caro Quintero. He was the brother of Félix Gallardo's imprisoned associate Rafael Caro Quintero. Miguel's operation became known as the Sonora Cartel.

Shipment of drugs along the Gulf coast of Mexico, including the highly populated border crossing area between Matamoros, Mexico, and Brownsville, Texas, would be run by Juan García Ábrego. He was a drug lord with links to the Cali Cartel, whose power and political connections were nearly equal to Félix Gallardo's. His organization would become known as the Gulf Cartel.

The trafficking of drugs from cities on Mexico's Pacific coast was given to an organization headed by two of Félix Gallardo's most trusted associates: Joaquín Guzmán Loera and Ismael Zambada García. Both men had been involved in coordinating the Guadalajara Cartel's shipments of cocaine from Colombia. They had proven themselves to be experts at the logistics of smuggling large quantities of drugs on cargo ships and commercial airplanes. Their organization became known as the Sinaloa Cartel.

Félix Gallardo's plan to organize the Mexican drug routes among subordinates worked out well for several years. Authorities finally caught up with Félix Gallardo in 1989. He was arrested, charged with drug trafficking and murder, and sentenced to 40 years in a Mexican prison. For a few years he was able to remain involved in smuggling activities, communicating with the cartels with a cell phone from his jail cell. In 1991, when Félix Gallardo was transferred to a maximum security prison, he was no longer able to take an active role in drug smuggling operations.

From this point, the major Mexican drug cartels operated independently. Sometimes they worked together; more often they fought with rival cartels to expand their operations. Any time a cartel leader died or was arrested, other groups would attempt to move in and take over that cartel's drug smuggling routes. Throughout the 1990s, the Mexican drug cartels gained power, particularly as the strength of the Colombian cartels declined.

The Mexican government did little to stop the activities of drug cartels during the 1990s. The most powerful political party in Mexico, Partido Revolucionario Institucional (PRI), was extremely corrupt. PRI had ruled the country since the late 1920s, and often resorted to electoral fraud in order to remain in power. Bribery was simply the way things were done in Mexico. Government officials, police officers, judges, and others were all on the payroll of the drug lords.

This is not to say that Mexican authorities did not take action against drug cartels. Sometimes, the violence associated with drug traffickers grew so bad that the Mexican people pressured the government to take action. In other instances, corrupt local police were drawn into the rivalries between Mexican cartels, supporting the group that paid the highest bribes.

Sometimes, cartel leaders would use the authorities to weaken or eliminate a rival. They would inform local police about the whereabouts of key members of another cartel, or tell drug agents where they could intercept an enemy's drug shipments. The resulting arrests would disrupt the rival cartel's business, creating a power vacuum that could be exploited.

Even when a drug lord was sent to prison, he was often able to continue running his cartel. For example, Sinaloa Cartel boss Joaquín Guzmán was arrested in 1993 and sentenced to 20 years in prison. However, he was able to maintain control by passing messages to underlings through family members who visited him in prison.

One of the biggest fears of Mexican drug lords was that they would be extradited to the United States if they had been indicted for drug trafficking or other crimes in an American court. In an American prison, they would not have the same freedom or status that they had in Mexican jails. Cash from the cartels flowed to corrupt government officials to ensure that the drug dealers would not be imprisoned outside of Mexico. The government leaders pocketed the bribes and refused to extradite criminals to the U.S., arguing that they should serve their sentences in Mexican prisons first.

Even millions in bribes couldn't protect Gulf Cartel leader Juan García Ábrego, however. By 1994, the Gulf Cartel had become so powerful that Ábrego was included on the FBI's "Ten Most Wanted" list—the first drug smuggler to achieve this dubious honor. He was captured by Mexican police the next year and extradited to the United States, where he was convicted of money laundering and drug trafficking. Ábrego was sentenced to 11 life terms, which he is currently serving in a maximum-security prison in Colorado. A subsequent U.S. investigation found that during 1993–94 the Gulf Cartel had paid more than $9 million to a high-ranking Mexican official in charge of the federal police, Mario Ruiz Massieu, and to family members of former Mexican president Carlos Salinas, in a failed effort to keep Ábrego from being extradited.

Ábrego was the exception, rather than the rule, during the 1990s, however. The Gulf Cartel floundered after his arrest, as several people fought to gain control of the organization. Osiel Cárdenas emerged as the leader of the Gulf Cartel in 1999. To ensure he would stay in power, Cárdenas created a paramilitary organization called Los Zetas. He hired many former Mexican soldiers and policemen, paying them much higher wages than they had earned working for the government. Originally, the group served as bodyguards, but they soon began attacking members of rival cartels so that the Gulf Cartel could muscle in on new trafficking routes. The other cartels began to arm themselves more heavily as well, leading to a rise in gang warfare.

The situation in Mexico began to change after the July 2000 election of

Members of the Mexico's Policía Federal Preventiva— more commonly known as the *federales*, or federal police— wait for orders in the violence-ridden border city of Ciudad Juárez, February 2009. The federal police were formed in 1999 specifically to combat the drug cartels. Government authorities had found that local police were often on the payrolls of the drug cartels, and could not be relied on to fight the war on drugs.

Vicente Fox as president. Fox, who had campaigned on a promise to end corruption in government, was the first non-PRI president in 70 years. During his six-year term, Fox was more willing than his predecessors had been to work with American drug agencies like the DEA. As a result, Mexican federal police arrested several important cartel leaders. In 2002, they weakened the Tijuana Cartel by capturing Benjamín Arellano Félix and killing Ramón Arellano Félix in a gun fight. The next year, Gulf Cartel leader Osiel Cárdenas was arrested in the border city of Matamoros.

President Fox also agreed to extradite drug lords to the United States. He sent dozens of imprisoned criminals to the United States.

One who avoided extradition was Joaquín Guzmán. When he learned that the Fox administration was changing Mexico's extradition policy, the Sinaloa Cartel boss managed to escape from prison in a laundry van. He returned to western Mexico.

The arrests and pressure from the Mexican government led to an increase in fighting among the drug cartels as they sought to expand their turf. After the arrest of Cárdenas, Guzmán took aim at the Gulf Cartel, which he believed to be weakened. He sent well-armed enforcers

Joaquín Guzmán

led by the four Beltrán Leyva brothers to fight for control of the Gulf Cartel's crossings on the Texas-Mexico border. This resulted in heavy fighting and the establishment of a new drug cartel known as the Beltrán Leyva organization.

Guzmán also made aggressive inroads into Baja California, where the Tijuana Cartel had been weakened by a power struggle. Fighting between the Tijuana and Sinaloa cartels in 2005, along with the rise of an extremely violent new organization called La Familia Michoacána on Mexico's Pacific coast, led to a significant increase in the murder rate. This in turn resulted in greater efforts by Mexican federal police to crack down on drug cartels.

In 2006 Tijuana Cartel leader Francisco Rafael Arellano Félix was arrested by the U.S. Coast Guard. His arrest led to a power vacuum that rivals for the cartel's leadership tried to exploit. That same year, dozens of other Mexican drug lords were extradited to the U.S. to face justice at the end of Fox's presidential term. Overall, however, drug gang violence increased in 2006, with more than 2,300 murders attributed to the cartels and numerous reports of people tortured or beheaded for opposing the cartels.

In December 2006 Fox's newly elected successor as president, Felipe Calderón, intensified the government's war on the drug cartels. He sent 6,500 Mexican soldiers and federal police to the state of Michoacán—Calderón's home state—to stop the violence of groups like La Familia Michoacána. The move had the opposite effect. Violence increased as government troops and cartel solders became involved in gun battles on the streets of Morelia, Uruapan, Zamora, and the port of Lázaro Cárdenas. The conflict soon spread to other parts of Mexico, with additional federal troops sent to Ciudad Juárez and Tijuana, as well as the states of Chihuahua, Durango, and Sinaloa.

In 2007, the U.S. government promised to help Mexico fight the drug cartels by providing $1.4 billion for equipment and police training. That same year Mexico extradited more than 100 high-ranking cartel leaders to the United States, including Osiel Cárdenas.

During 2008 and 2009, Guzmán led the Sinaloa Cartel into a war for control of Ciudad Juárez. The Juárez Cartel fought back savagely, and the city quickly became the drug war's bloodiest battleground. President Calderón soon sent an additional 10,000 troops to Ciudad Juárez, but they could not prevent the killings. The violence even spilled over the border into Arizona, with several murders by armed gangs related to the

Felipe Calderón's decision to send the Mexican military to fight against drug cartels may have had the unwanted consequence of increasing the violence. Today, the country's murder rate is among the ten highest in the world.

cartel conflict. The body count continued to increase, with more than 6,300 Mexicans killed in drug-related violence during 2008, and over 7,000 killed in 2009.

Authorities did have some successes in the fight against the cartels. In 2008, Tijuana Cartel boss Eduardo Arellano Félix was arrested in Mexico. This would touch off a power struggle within the cartel. However, the government's biggest success came in December 2009, when drug lord Arturo Beltran Leyva

Eduardo Arellano Félix

American Guns and Mexican Drug Violence

One reason for the violence of Mexico's war on drugs is that the cartels have become increasingly well-armed. This is due in part from the availability of military-grade weapons, such as rocket-propelled grenades and handheld surface-to-air missiles, from criminal organizations like the Russian mafiya. But the easy availability of automatic weapons and assault rifles in the United States also contributes to the problem. Mexico has fairly strict laws regulating gun ownership, making it difficult for people to purchase weapons in the country. It is much easier to buy guns in the United States, and data from the Bureau of Alcohol, Tobacco, and Firearms (ATF) indicates that many cartels are doing just that. Studies based on ATF data, as well as information provided by the Mexican government, have indicated that roughly 75 percent of weapons captured by Mexican police after being used to commit crimes had originally been purchased in the U.S. During a March 2009 visit to Mexico, U.S. Secretary of State Hillary Rodham Clinton said, "Our inability to prevent weapons from being illegally smuggled across the border to arm these criminals causes the deaths of police, of soldiers and civilians."

In May 2010, Mexican President Felipe Calderón addressed the U.S. Congress and suggested that it should consider reinstating a ban on semi-automatic assault weapons and large-capacity magazines. These weapons had been outlawed in 1994; Calderón claimed that the increase in Mexican drug cartel violence coincided with the expiration of the U.S. legal ban in 2004. "I understand that the purpose of the Second Amendment is to guarantee good American citizens the ability to defend themselves and their nation," Calderón told Congress. "But believe me, many of these guns are not going to honest American hands."

The U.S. government has sometimes been more a part of the problem than the solution. Between 2007 and 2011 ATF agents conducted several operations attempting to track illegally purchased guns to Mexican drug cartels. They used an approach known as "gun-walking," in which they allowed licensed American firearms dealers to sell weapons to people suspected of being linked to drug traffickers. The plan was to track the firearms as they were transferred to higher-level drug dealers or cartel leaders. ATF agents hoped this would provide evidence leading to the arrests of cartel bosses, which would weaken the cartel and disrupt its activities. They also wanted to break up organizations that were purchasing American guns and smuggling them into Mexico.

Unfortunately, it turned out that the ATF was unable to track all of the weapons. In one operation that ran from 2009 to 2011, nicknamed "Fast and Furious," the agents allowed more than 2,000 weapons to be sold to suspicious buyers, but could only track about 700 of them. Some of these weapons were not found until after they had been used in drug-related crimes, including the murder of an American border patrol agent named Brian Terry and the killings of more than 150 Mexican civilians. Most of the weapons went to the Sinaloa Cartel; some were sold to La Familia. The gunwalking programs did not lead to drug lord arrests or weaken the cartels, so the ATF shut them down. However, Operation Fast and Furious became a major embarrassment for the Obama administration in 2012.

and six of his bodyguards were killed during a shootout with Mexican police. The cartel immediately responded by killing family members of a soldier who had participated in the raid, and fire-bombing a school to warn others not to interfere in cartel affairs. However, without Arturo to run things, the Beltran Leyva smuggling organization was no longer effective.

Another major arrest came in January 2010, when police captured Teodoro "El Teo" Garcia, a feared leader of the Tijuana Cartel who was known for having rivals tortured, killed, and dissolved in acid.

Soon after this, the major remaining cartels in Mexico began to form alliances. One faction included the Juárez Cartel, Tijuana Cartel, and Los Zetas, which had broken away from the Gulf Cartel to become a fully independent drug trafficking organization. The other faction included the Gulf Cartel and the Sinaloa Cartel, along with remnants of La Familia Michoacána that were now calling themselves the Knights Templar.

By 2013, more than 50,000 Mexican soldiers and 35,000 federal police were fighting the drug war against the cartels. They were receiving assistance from the DEA and other American agencies. Government officials on both sides of the border have said they remain committed to stopping the violence and stemming the flow of drugs heading north and guns and cash heading south. Yet the movement of drugs into the United States continues practically unabated, and the violence in Mexico has shown little sign of slowing down, with death tolls of roughly 20,000 per year over the three previous years.

Federal police stop a suspected cartel soldier in the border city of Ciudad Juárez. By 2009, this city on the U.S.-Mexico border had the world's highest murder rate.

Amado Carrillo Fuentes

Mexican Lord of the Skies

In November of 1997, the bodies of three medical doctors were discovered at the side of a highway between Mexico City and Acapulco. The bodies had been stuffed into steel oil drums and encased in concrete. After an investigation, Mexican police learned that four months earlier, the physicians had performed an operation in Mexico City. Their patient was Amado Carrillo Fuentes, one of Mexico's wealthiest drug lords. Carrillo had died on the operating table.

When it comes to death in the world of illegal drug trafficking, there are often many unanswered questions. Had the doctors deliberately killed Carrillo during the operation, and been tortured and murdered in retaliation? Although this seemed likely, police could not be absolutely sure. The only thing that was certain, however, was that one of the most powerful and innovative drug traf-

fickers in Mexican history was dead.

Amado Carrillo Fuentes was born in 1956, in the Mexican state of Sinaloa. His father owned land but was not particularly rich. Amado wanted to be rich, though. He dropped out of school after the sixth grade and left his hometown, telling everyone that he wouldn't come back until he was wealthy.

Drug trafficking seemed like a fast, though dangerous, way to get rich, and young Carrillo had an uncle who was involved in the drug trade. Ernesto Fonseca Carrillo, a smuggler who eventually became the leader of the Guadalajara Cartel, opened the door to drug trafficking for his nephew. Uncle Ernesto got Amado a position harvesting opium poppies, and began to teach him the smuggling business.

By the 1980s, the drug trade was undergoing major changes. There was a crackdown on Colombian drug cartels, but the market in the U.S. for cocaine, methamphetamines, heroin, and marijuana was as strong—and lucrative—as ever. The weakening of the Colombian cartels gave Mexican drug traffickers an opportunity to take a larger share of the drug market. Drugs from Central and South America were now shipped north to Mexico, closer to the U.S. border, and the Mexican drug cartels took charge of the traffic.

During the mid-1980s, Ernesto Fonseca sent Amado Carrillo to the Mexican state of Chihuahua. There, he joined a drug ring called the Juárez Cartel, which worked with the Medellín Cartel to receive shipments of cocaine from Colombia.

The Juárez Cartel was based in Ciudad Juárez, just a few miles from the Texas border town of El Paso. It had been founded in the late 1970s by Rafael Aguilar Guajardo, a former police officer who used his connections to protect his criminal empire. Because of Carrillo's intelligence and family background, he soon became Guajardo's second in command. Carrillo helped to oversee shipments and directed operations to smuggle them across the border into the United States. By the early 1990s, the Juárez Cartel was the wealthiest drug cartel in Mexico.

Due to his success, Guajardo was targeted by Mexican police. They attempted to arrest him in 1992, and

Case File

Amado Carrillo Fuentes

Born: *December 17, 1956*

Known for: *innovative smuggler who used a fleet of airplanes to move drugs from Mexico to the United States and other countries. Leader of the Juárez Cartel from 1993 to 1997, Carrillo is thought to have amassed a personal fortune in excess of $25 billion.*

Died: *July 3, 1997, during an operation to change his appearance.*

siezed several properties that he owned. Allegedly, to avoid arrest Guajardo offered to reveal the names of the some government and police officials who were working with the Juárez Cartel. This could have endangered the entire Juárez Cartel, so in April 1993, while the drug kingpin was on vacation in Cancun, Guajardo was gunned down in front of his family. It is widely believed that Amado Carrillo had ordered the assassination.

Amado Carrillo took over command of the Juárez Cartel at a good time. In the mid-1990s the leaders of other powerful Mexican drug gangs, such as the Gulf Cartel and the Sinaloa Cartel, had either been arrested, forced into hiding,

In 1981 Carrillo used some of his profits from drug trafficking to start an air shipping business under an assumed name. By the 1990s he controlled a fleet of more than two dozen cargo planes, including Boeing 727s, Lear jets, and Caravelle jetliners. He used these planes to secretly deliver tons of cocaine to his clients around the world.

or killed. This created an opportunity for the Juárez Cartel to expand into territories that those rival groups had once controlled. Soon the Juárez Cartel controlled most of the drug trafficking along the U.S.-Texas border, and the DEA considered Carrillo to be Mexico's biggest drug kingpin.

Carrillo believed in running his drug cartel like a business. He brought new levels of creativity and discipline to drug trafficking. Under his leadership, the Juárez Cartel used modern technology to conduct counter-surveillance against law enforcement officials and rival cartels. Carrillo purchased large tracts of real estate so his organization could operate in many different places. Most famously, he bought and used a fleet of jetliners to fly cocaine into the United States. This led people to nickname the drug lord *El Señor de los Cielos*—"the Lord of the Skies."

As powerful as he was, Amado Carrillo wanted even more power. Colombia was still the world's major supplier of cocaine, but by the mid-1990s the cartels had been weakened by arrests. Carrillo took advantage by offering a new business plan: the Colombians could bring their cocaine to Mexico, where they would be paid for it in cash. The Juárez Cartel would take care of smuggling the drugs into the United States and distributing them. The Colombians agreed. This arrangement gave the Juárez Cartel almost total control of the cocaine trade in the U.S.

Like his former boss and mentor Guajardo, Carrillo was careful to cultivate a network of supporters within the Mexican government. He paid off police officers and government officials. Carrillo even forged an alliance with General José de Jesús Gutiérrez, the head of Mexico's anti-drug operations. This was a major coup. With General Gutiérrez on his payroll, Carrillo could not only evade Mexican authorities, he could also make sure that the Mexican government focused its drug-war resources on rival cartels, leaving a larger share of the business for the Juárez Cartel. It was even rumored that Carrillo had connections to Carlos Salinas, president of Mexico from 1988

to 1994. "Amado [Carrillo] is committed to large-scale operations with tremendous protection—better even than Juan García Ábrego [head of the Gulf Cartel] could get," a Mexican drug investigator told the *Los Angeles Times* in 1995. "His operations cannot be done without the direct complicity of the highest levels of protection from politicians and from the police and counter-narcotics agencies. He is a top-level narcotics trafficker. . . . The facts have shown us that he is the boss."

Carrillo's business savvy did not mean he was not also a ruthless criminal. He was perfectly willing to combine

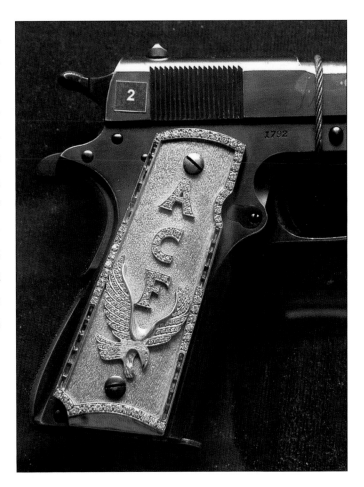

This handgun once owned by Amado Carrillo, and bearing the drug lord's initials, features a gold plate encrusted with diamonds and emeralds on the handle.

Various photos of Amado Carrillo Fuentes, who often tried to change his appearance in order to evade capture by police.

modern corporate techniques with old-fashioned, gangland brutality. At least 400 murders were linked to the Juárez Cartel during the time Carrillo was in charge—there probably were many other killings, but these are the only ones for which authorities had strong evidence that linked him to the crimes. Enemies of the cartel were often found beheaded. Carrillo thought nothing of killing police officers, and sometimes had their children murdered as a warning to others not to interfere with his activities. If any of Carrillo's men lost a shipment of drugs that had already been paid for, they knew they would die.

Throughout his reign, Carrillo was careful to make another kind of connection. He knew that much of his power depended on not alienating ordinary Mexicans. To earn their admiration and loyalty, he threw great parties in his home village. He had basketball courts built for children and constructed other popular sports venues. When a village church needed renovations, Carrillo provided the funds. He frequently paid medical expenses for poor people and

Vicente Carrillo Fuentes is currently at large. He is on the FBI's "most wanted" list, with a $5 million reward offered for his capture. The Juárez Cartel leader has been indicted for drug trafficking, murder, and other criminal acts by a U.S. federal court in Texas.

employed many regular people in his home state. As a result many Mexicans turned a blind eye to his brutality and focused instead on the generous things he did to buy their loyalty.

With his combination of cleverness and cruelty, Carrillo made himself and his cartel phenomenally rich. At its height the organization was making tens of millions of dollars a week. It's believed that by 1997 Carrillo was worth about $25 billion.

However, Carrillo acquired notoriety along with his power and wealth. In early 1997 he lost his protection when Mexican officials began investigating General Gutiérrez for corruption. (Gutiérrez was eventually convicted of various crimes related to drug trafficking.) Soon Carrillo was being zealously hunted by American and Mexican police. His group's incursion into areas traditionally controlled by other cartels had also made him enemies. Carrillo was a wanted man and no place seemed safe.

Desperate to evade capture, Carrillo went to Mexico City with a plan. He would have plastic surgery to alter his appearance so the authorities and his

enemies could not find him. However, Carrillo did not survive the eight-hour procedure.

At first, the Mexican government was not sure whether the dead man was Carrillo. Rumors spread that Carrillo had planted the story of his death so he could escape. Those rumors persist even today. However, DNA testing confirmed that the dead man was indeed Amado Carrillo.

With the death of Amado Carrillo Fuentes, the Juárez Cartel began to decline. The drug kingpin's brother, Vicente Carrillo Fuentes, took over as leader of the cartel. The Juárez Cartel became involved in turf wars with another cartels during the 2000s. Fighting was particularly vicious between the Juárez and Sinaloa cartels from 2004 to 2005 and from 2007 to the present.

La Familia Michoacána

Murder, Myth, and Meth

One night in September 2006, members of a Mexican gang called La Familia Michoacána walked into a night club in Uruapan, Michoacán. They spun five severed heads across the dance floor in full view of the club's horrified patrons. The gang members vanished into the darkness, leaving behind a message that read: "La Familia doesn't kill for money, it doesn't kill women, it doesn't kill innocent people—only those who deserve to die. Everyone should know: this is divine justice."

According to reports that surfaced later, the men to whom the heads belonged had murdered a waitress who had been romantically involved with a member of the gang. This sort of gruesome reprisal was typical of La Familia, a violent Mexican street gang and drug cartel. Beheading—of police and soldiers, rival gang members, politicians,

journalists, and even members who violated the gang's strict rules—was among La Familia's favorite tactics to instill terror and ensure its control over drug trafficking and organized crime.

La Familia emerged in Michoacán, a state in western Mexico on the Pacific coast, during the 1980s. At one time the gang—then called La Empresa—was associated with the Gulf Cartel. La Empresa's founder, Carlos Rosales Mendoza, was friendly with Gulf Cartel leader Osiel Cárdenas. In the late 1990s, Cárdenas sent members of the Gulf Cartel's paramilitary wing, Los Zetas, to Michoacán, where they helped Rosales and La Familia take control over drug trafficking in the region from a rival cartel.

La Empresa practiced many of the traditional activities of organized crime syndicates, such as extortion and kidnappings for ransom. The organization charged "protection fees" from at least 85 percent of the legal businesses in Michoacán. Mining companies had to pay the gang a "tax" of $1.50 per ton on the metals they produced, while cattle ranchers were charged a dollar for every kilogram of meat they sold. Other victims of their protection rackets included the region's prosperous lime and avocado farms, and the promoters of bullfights, concerts, and other sporting events.

Above all, however, La Empresa was in the business of manufacturing and selling drugs. Marijuana and opium poppies had been grown in Michoacán for generations. The gang took over processing of poppy sap into heroin and arranged shipments of the drugs into the United States. They also made deals to smuggle Colombian cocaine into the United States.

Michoacán became a starting point for smugglers. Boats carrying drug shipments could be launched from the multitude of tiny bays on Michoacán's rugged Pacific coastline. The busy seaport of Lázaro Cárdenas could also be used to receive cocaine from South America and send drugs to American cities like Los Angeles, San Diego, and San Francisco, as well as to ports in Asia.

Because Michoacán is relatively far from the U.S. border, the cartel made partnerships with other gangs so that its trucks could pass through their territory. These refrigerated trucks would be packed with fruits and vegetables grown in Michoacán, headed to U.S. supermarkets in major cities like Atlanta, Dallas, and Los Angeles. Drugs would be hidden in secret compartments, and distributed from those cities by gang

Packets of cocaine hidden inside the fuel tank of the Mexican vessel *Xoloescuintle*. The ship set out from Lázaro Cárdenas carrying the drug shipment in August 1999. *Xoloescuintle* was stopped by a U.S. Coast Guard cutter while it was traveling north along Mexico's Pacific coast. After searching the vessel, the Coast Guard boarding team removed 10.5 tons of cocaine from the fuel tanks.

This container of crystal meth was discovered by the DEA during a raid of a La Familia drug distribution center in 2009. The Mexican cartel became known for providing large quantities of high-quality crystal meth to dealers in the United States, particularly in the southwest, midwest, and south.

members throughout the United States.

The gang's most important source of revenue soon became crystal methamphetamine. This drug became extremely popular among users in the American southwest during the 1990s. The drug can be "cooked" in small makeshift laboratories, using a variety of household chemicals and solvents. Production of crystal meth creates toxic chemicals, and the drug itself is highly addictive and causes serious health problems. In response to the growing meth problem, in the late 1990s and early 2000s the U.S. government passed a number of laws aimed at regulating ingredients critical to meth productions, such as cold medicines and other products that contain the drug pseudoephedrine.

The American crackdown on meth production created a profitable new opportunity for Mexican drug cartels.

Large amounts of pseudoephedrine could still be legally imported to Mexico, and La Empresa set up numerous meth labs to produce *cristal*, as the drug is called in Spanish. Some of these labs were set up in industrial area near the port of Lázaro Cárdenas, where pseudoephedrine shipments from Asia could be quickly processed into meth. However, most meth labs were established in the remote, rugged mountains that cover a considerable portion of Michoacán. This made it hard for Mexican police to find the operations and shut them down.

In 2004, Mexican authorities arrested Carlos Rosales, and Nazario Moreno González seized control of the gang. Moreno was known as El Mas Loco ("The Craziest One"), and he brought to the gang—now called La Familia Michoacána—a strange new religious emphasis. He insisted that gang members should attend church services, and distributed bibles throughout the state. Gang members were also expected to stay clean and not use drugs or alcohol. La Familia earned support from poor people in Michoacán because it used some of the profits from its illegal activity to fund schools, food pantries, and other community services. It also used drug money to bribe local officials and judges, ensuring that the gang could continue to operate without scrutiny.

Given Moreno's religious belief it may seem strange that he was involved in drug production, smuggling, and dealing. The cartel leader attempted to justify his gang's actions by claiming that their product was only intended for export to the United States and other countries. Moreno and his supporters also noted that the cartel was paying local people more to produce drugs than they could earn in legitimate businesses.

The chapel of Jesús del Monte is located in Tlalpujahua, a village in northeastern Michoacán. According to a 2010 report on the gang published by the Strategic Studies Institute of the U.S. Army War College, this area was used by the cartel to train some of its most dangerous members. "Those who show an aptitude for violence are taken in groups of 40 to a wilderness area known as the Jesús del Monte," notes the report. "There, they are directed to shoot, butcher, and cook 15 victims to demonstrate that they are neither squeamish about killing innocents nor repulsed by handling bloody body parts. The leaders of La Familia . . . assure those who successfully complete this exercise that they are prepared to do the Lord's work—that is, safeguarding women, combatting competing cartels, and preventing the local sale of drugs."

Case File

Nazario Moreno González

Born: *March 8, 1970*

Known for: *took control of La Familia Michoacána in 2004 and turned the group into one of the most powerful and violent drug cartels in Mexico; preached a strange quasi-religious message and claimed to seek social justice for the people of Michoacán.*

Died: *December 9, 2010, in a shootout with Mexican police*

Residents of Michoacán came to believe that the gang was more effective at maintaining order than the corrupt local police. Gang members tortured or killed thieves, prostitutes, drug addicts, low-level drug dealers, and other "undesirables"—such as the men who had assaulted the waitress in Uruapan during 2006. The gang made it clear that such people were not welcome in their community, and reduced the rate of certain crimes as a result.

Violent crime levels rose overall, however, as La Familia's founder claimed that beatings and killings were not just acceptable, they were "divine justice." The gang dealt harshly with members who broke La Familia's rigid rules of personal conduct, or made a mistake that resulted in the loss of a drug shipment. The first and second offenses resulted in severe beatings. A third mistake meant the offender was executed. The organization also kept close tabs on its members' families. If gang leaders suspected a person was trying to leave La Familia or was going to inform on the organization, the person's family was likely to suffer.

Nazario Moreno and his top lieutenants, Arnoldo Rueda Medina, Rafael Cedeño Hernández, and José de Jesús Méndez Vargas, ended La Familia's association with the Gulf Cartel in 2004. The two organizations soon began fighting a gang war for control of drug activities in Michoacán.

La Familia grew quickly as an independent organization, and within a few years the gang had roughly 4,000 members operating in Mexico and the United States. La Familia Michoacána set up networks to distribute drugs throughout the United States, particularly in the American southwest and midwest where demand for crystal meth was highest. By 2006, when Felipe Calderón became president of Mexico, the cartel was believed to be earning more than $5 billion a year from its illegal activities, and had expanded its turf into the neighboring Mexican states of Guerrero and Guanajuato.

Calderón, a native of Michoacán,

decided to send federal troops into his home state to stop the violent conflict between La Familia, the Gulf Cartel, and other Mexican drug trafficking organizations. This started the Mexican war on drugs. The violence rose dramatically as government agents fought with cartel soldiers and attempted to shut down illegal labs and smuggling operations.

In April 2009, Mexican authorities arrested a number of cartel members, including Rafael Cedeño, who was considered to be Nazario Moreno's second-in-command. The next month, federal police arrested more than two dozen judges and city officials in Michoacán, accusing them of taking bribes from La Familia and other drug traffickers.

In July 2009, Mexican authorities arrested Arnoldo Rueda. The next day, gang members armed with grenades and machine guns attacked Mexican army units and federal police in eight cities in Michoacán. In one particularly brutal attack a few days later, a dozen Mexican police officers were kidnapped; they were tied up and executed. A sign left with their bodies warned federal authorities, *Vengan por otro, los estamos esperando* ("Come for another of our leaders, we are waiting for you.").

American drug agencies were also interested in bringing down the cartel. In October 2009, the DEA, FBI, and the Bureau of Alcohol, Tobacco, and Firearms (ATF) ended a four-year-long investigation with a series of raids of La Familia operations in the United States. Dubbed Project Coronado, the operation resulted in the arrest of more than 300 people in 19 U.S. states. Authorities confiscated more than 725 pounds of methamphetamine, 139 pounds (62 kilos) of cocaine, and nearly 1,000 pounds of marijuana. The haul also

The July 2009 arrest of Arnoldo Rueda touched off a series of violent attacks by La Familia on federal police in Mexico. The attacks killed 17 federal police and soldiers, wounding more than 20 others. They led to further conflict between government forces and drug cartels in the Michoacán region. Today, Rueda remains in Mexico's maximum security Altiplano prison, where many other captured drug lords are also being held.

Weapons and cash seized by American authorities during the Project Coronado arrests in October 2009.

tinued doing business with few changes.

American and Mexican authorities continued to focus on La Familia, however. By 2010 more than 1,100 cartel members had been arrested, and over $100 million in drugs, cash, and weapons had been seized. In December of that year, cartel leader Nazario Moreno was killed in a village in Michoacán during a raid by federal police.

In June 2011, Mexican officials captured José de Jesús Méndez, who had taken over the cartel after Moreno's death. After this the Mexican government declared that La Familia Michoacána was no longer operative because most of the cartel's leaders had been killed, arrested, or driven into hiding in the mountains.

In early 2013, a new wave of violence claimed dozens of lives. It was blamed on the successor to La Familia, a group known as the Caballeros Templarios (or Knights Templar). This group is run by a former La Familia leader named Servando Gómez Martínez. It has taken over the La Familia's drug operations in Michoacán, Guerrero, and other states, and continues to espouse the parent cartel's strange religious message. As a result, despite the extinction of one of Mexico's most violent drug cartels, the prospects for peace in the Michoacán region appear to have dimmed.

included $3.4 million in U.S. currency, more than a hundred vehicles, and nearly 150 weapons. "We have dealt a substantial blow to a group that has polluted our neighborhoods with illicit drugs and has terrorized Mexico with unimaginable violence," said FBI Director Robert S. Mueller.

The truth, however, is that this major bust had little immediate effect on La Familia's operations. The lost cash and drugs were little more than pocket change to the multi-billion-dollar organization. Many members of the cartel weren't even aware of the bust, and con-

Mara Salvatrucha

Violent Salvadoran Street Gang

Among the countless street gangs that have infested America's cities, none has ever metastasized to the same degree as Mara Salvatrucha. In the early 1980s, when it was formed, the gang operated in a few Los Angeles barrios. Just three decades later, in 2012, the U.S. government designated Mara Salvatrucha a transnational criminal organization, deemed to pose an "unusual and extraordinary threat to the national security, foreign policy and economy of the United States." The gang is a major player in the drug trade. It is also involved in a range of other criminal activities, from blackmail and extortion to kidnapping, sex trafficking, and contract murder. Mara Salvatrucha is believed to have about 10,000 members in the United States, and perhaps 25,000 in the Central American nations of El Salvador, Guatemala, and Honduras. It has a significant and expanding presence in Mexico. It is also present in Canada.

The roots of Mara Salvatrucha, also known as MS-13, lie in tiny El Salvador. In 1979 civil war broke out in the country, which at the time had a population of about 4.5 million. The Salvadoran army battled a leftist insurgent group known as the Farabundo Marti National Liberation Front, or FMLN. Right-wing death squads kidnapped and murdered thousands of civilians suspected of sympathizing with the FMLN. The brutal conflict would last for a dozen years and claim the lives of an estimated 75,000 people. About a million Salvadoran refugees fled to the United States. Many settled in Southern California.

In Los Angeles, newly arrived Salvadorans were victimized by established street gangs, especially Mexican-

American gangs. In the Pico-Union neighborhood, Salvadoran youths formed Mara Salvatrucha to protect themselves. Many of the original members had trained and fought with the FMLN guerrillas, and the gang quickly earned a reputation for viciousness. "In [El Salvador], we were taught to kill our own people, no matter if they were from your own blood," explained Ernesto

Members of MS-13 are often heavily tattooed. This clique leader was arrested in a 2008 crackdown.

Miranda, a cofounder of MS-13. "If your father was the enemy, you had to kill him. So the training we got during the war in our country served to make us one of the most violent gangs in the United States."

The gang's name speaks both to its history and to ethnic pride. The word *mara* means "gang" or "clique." *Salvatrucha* has been interpreted several ways. Some say the term refers to a specific group of guerrillas who fought in El Salvador's civil war. Others more simply view the word as a colloquial term for a Salvadoran man. In a court case brought against several MS-13 members in 2008, the federal government said the term was a combination of *salva*, short for "Salvadoran"; and *trucha*, a slang term meaning "fear us," "look out," or "heads up."

The significance of "13" has also been explained in different ways. One common explanation is that the number refers to M, the 13th letter of the alphabet, and that the gang adopted it as a sign of allegiance to the Mexican Mafia. Also known as "La Eme," the Mexican Mafia is the dominant Latino prison gang in California. In the early 1990s, Mara Salvatrucha agreed to pay to the Mexican Mafia a "tax" on profits from its illegal activities (largely the sale of crack cocaine). In exchange, the Mexican Mafia would offer protection to incarcerated members of MS-13.

Mara Salvatrucha had by this time spread beyond the borders of California into other states. U.S. immigration policy would soon have the unintended consequence of making the gang an international organization.

After peace accords signed in 1992 finally ended El Salvador's civil war, the U.S. government withdrew asylum status for Salvadorans. This paved the way for the deportation of those in the country without proper documents, and for those who had documents but weren't citizens and had been convicted of a serious crime. At first, relatively small numbers of Salvadorans—most of them gang members imprisoned for serious crimes—were sent back to El Salvador. Some of them decided to establish Mara Salvatrucha in the country of their birth.

Their efforts got a huge boost with the passage of the Illegal Immigration Reform and Immigrant Responsibility Act of 1996. Under the law, which mandated the deportation of noncitizens even for minor offenses, thousands of Salvadoran immigrants were deported. Many had come to the United States as young children and had no ties in El Salvador. They were readily pulled into MS-13.

El Salvador's weak police force and criminal justice system were ill equipped to deal with the appearance of a large, ruthless gang. MS-13 spread rapidly through El Salvador and soon moved into neighboring Honduras and Guatemala. Each of these countries saw spikes in violent crime.

Meanwhile, MS-13 leaders in El Salvador maintained contact with groups in the United States. But beyond ordering the U.S.-based groups to remit money to them, they made little effort to oversee operations in El Norte.

In the United States, MS-13 had never had a defined national leadership structure. Instead, it was a network of loosely affiliated groups, or cliques, each with its own hierarchy. The cliques shared a common gang culture and followed the same core rules, but they didn't typically coordinate their activities. In recent years, however, that may have begun to change.

As of 2012, MS-13 cliques were believed to be operating in 46 states. Many cliques extort protection money from local businesses owned by Salvadoran or other Central American immigrants. The trafficking of illicit drugs, including cocaine, heroin, and methamphetamine, is another major source of revenue. MS-13 cliques often run prostitution rings as well.

Mara Salvatrucha's motto *mata, roba, viola, controla*—"kill, steal, rape, control"—hints at its ruthlessness. Even by the standards of criminal gangs, MS-13 is notable for its barbarity. In the United States, members are infamous for hacking rivals to death with machetes. The gang's atrocities in Central America are legion, but perhaps none is more shocking than the December 2004 attack on a bus in Chamalecón, Honduras. MS-13 members forced the bus to the side of the road, then opened fire with AK-47 rifles. Twenty-eight passengers were killed, most of them women and children. A note left on the windshield warned government officials to abandon a crackdown on organized crime.

The gang's reputation for extreme violence made MS-13 members attractive foot soldiers for larger criminal syndicates. Mexico's warring drug cartels, including Los Zetas and the Sinaloa Cartel, reportedly hired MS-13 cliques as assassins and smugglers.

American officials recognized the growing threat presented by Mara Salvatrucha. In 2004 the FBI formed the MS-13 National Gang Task Force. The following year, the FBI coordinated an enforcement effort that swept up hundreds of gang members in the United States, El Salvador, Honduras, Guatemala, and Mexico.

A major investigation led to federal racketeering charges against 26 MS-13 members in 2008. In 2009 another

An infamous example of MS-13's willingness to commit violence came in December 2004, when six members of the gang armed with automatic rifles sprayed gunfire at this bus, which was carrying civilians in the town of Chamelecón, Honduras.

Drugs and guns seized in a DEA raid on an MS-13 clique.

investigation culminated in the seizure of large quantities of cocaine, heroin, and methamphetamine and the arrest of 20 MS-13 members. Many state and local law enforcement agencies brought cases against the gang as well. And between 2006 and 2012, the U.S. Department of Homeland Security arrested nearly 4,100 members of MS-13.

Despite all these efforts, MS-13's reach appeared to be extending. Increasing involvement in the drug trade seemed to be yielding larger and larger profits. And there were some troubling signs that MS-13 was moving toward a greater degree of centralized control.

The October 2012 designation of Mara Salvatrucha as a transnational criminal organization enabled the U.S. Department of the Treasury to freeze any identifiable assets of MS-13 members in the United States. The designation also made it illegal for American citizens and banks to conduct any trans-actions with MS-13. This, it was hoped, would cripple the gang financially before it began laundering money through legitimate U.S. businesses. "We want to prevent them from taking the next step," declared Special Agent James Hayes of U.S. Immigration and Customs Enforcement. "We want to prevent them from becoming the next global cartel." It remains to be seen whether that can be accomplished.

The Aryan Brotherhood

Drug Dealing in Federal Prisons

The Aryan Brotherhood may be synonymous with white supremacy and racial hatred, yet the notorious prison gang has proved surprisingly broad-minded where money is concerned. Behind the walls of American penitentiaries, the Brotherhood works with black associates to distribute illicit drugs to African-American inmates. Outside of prison, according to U.S. law enforcement officials, the Brotherhood has forged ties with Asian gangs to import heroin into the United States. And Brotherhood members are increasingly smuggling cocaine, methamphetamine, and weapons for Mexican drug cartels. "There's no doubt the Aryan Brotherhood are a bunch of racists," observed prison gang expert Tony Delgado, "but when it comes to doing business, the color that matters most to them isn't black or brown or white—it's green."

The Aryan Brotherhood wasn't always a moneymaking operation. White prisoners founded the gang as a means of self-protection.

Before the 1960s, most prisons in the United States were racially segregated. As that changed, racial violence became a big problem in many penitentiaries. One such institution was California's San Quentin State Prison, regarded as one of the toughest prisons in the country. In 1964 a new gang composed of Irish Americans began to form in San Quentin. The gang went by several names, including Diamond Tooth and Blue Bird. Its stated purpose was to protect its members from African-American and Latino prisoners, many of whom were already organized into their own gangs.

By 1967 the Diamond Tooth–Blue Bird gang had begun accepting whites who weren't of Irish extraction. It also

One indication that the United States is losing the war on drugs is the prevalence of illegal substances inside American prisons. Prisons have plenty of guards, security cameras, and regular searches of prisoners' belongings. Yet most experts agree that drugs like this crystal meth are readily available in federal prisons. Members of prison gangs like the Aryan Brotherhood arrange for drugs to be smuggled into the prisons and distributed to the convicts.

ably kill, a nonwhite inmate. The only way to leave was death. "If blacks attack whites, we send a message," said John Greschner, formerly one of the Aryan Brotherhood's top leaders, or "commissioners."

> We go pick one of their shot callers [leaders]. We catch them walking across the [prison] yard under guard escort in handcuffs. It don't matter. We're going to butcher him in handcuffs in front of God and everybody at high noon in the middle of the yard. And it's not just going to be a few clean stab marks. It's going to be a vicious, brutal killing. Because that's how brothers [AB members] take care of business, and a brother's work is never done.

This sort of violence can only go so far, however. During the 1970s, Aryan Brotherhood leaders came to the conclusion that to truly control San Quentin, they had to get involved in the business side of prison life. The money this would bring in would help the Brotherhood gain power and influence. As is often the case with gangs that want to make money, the Brotherhood turned to drug trafficking. Illegal drugs are a lucrative trade inside prison walls. The Brotherhood became a major supplier of drugs to the inmate population.

By the late 1970s, many Brotherhood members had been released from San Quentin, whether through parole or because they had served their full sentences. Once out,

merged with smaller white gangs, rebranding itself the Aryan Brotherhood.

The Aryan Brotherhood—also known as AB, Alice Baker, and the Brand—espoused a racist ideology borrowed from Adolf Hitler and the Nazis. Though smaller than rival ethnic gangs at San Quentin, it quickly became feared beyond its numbers. It accomplished this through extraordinary savagery. The only way to join the Aryan Brotherhood was to attack, and prefer-

Barry "The Barron" Mills (top) and Tyler "The Hulk" Bingham are believed to be the leaders of the Aryan Brotherhood's operations in the federal prison system. In 2006 they were indicted for drug trafficking and ordering the assault or murder of Brotherhood enemies and former gang members.

some of these men would move to new areas and make new connections. Often they would end up back in prison. In this manner, the Brotherhood spread to penitentiaries throughout the United States, and in 1980 a separate branch of the Aryan Brotherhood was founded for inmates in the federal prison system.

While they were outside of prison, Aryan Brotherhood members were expected to remain loyal to the gang. They had to turn over to gang leaders a percentage of any profit they made from illegal activities. Failure to do so would result in a "green light"—that is, a contract on the life of the offending member.

In the mid-1980s, the Aryan Brotherhood forged an alliance with a powerful Latino prison gang, the Mexican Mafia. Also known as La Eme, the Mexican Mafia had ties to a variety of criminal groups in Mexico. These included drug gangs that wanted buyers for cocaine and heroin throughout the United States. The Aryan Brotherhood had an increasingly large market to service, and the Mexican Mafia had the contacts to provide the necessary volume of drugs. A partnership made perfect sense from a business standpoint. Yet some observers expressed surprise that the Brotherhood would work so closely with people it supposedly despised as racially inferior.

Such cooperation has only expanded. Today the Brotherhood works not only with the Mexican Mafia but also with the Tijuana Cartel, one of Mexico's largest drug-trafficking organizations.

The Aryan Brotherhood may attract skinheads and other white supremacists with its message of racial hatred, and many of its 15,000 members and associates may actually believe that message. But the main purpose of the Brotherhood is to make money.

The Russian Mafiya
Guns, Drugs, and Money Laundering

In December of 1991, the Union of Soviet Socialist Republics dissolved, breaking into 14 separate, self-governing countries. Many people saw this enormous change as a victory for freedom and human rights. But the sudden end of the Communist system also led to confusion and poverty in Russia and the other nations that emerged from the centralized, top-down, government control of the Soviet system. One result of the loosening of government power was an upsurge in crime and corruption. Sophisticated criminal organizations began to spread and grow in strength.

Organized crime involves a collaboration among groups that are involved in illegal activities. These groups often model themselves and their management practices after legitimate, legal businesses. The word *mafia* is a Sicilian word that is often used to describe organized groups of criminals. Some of the most infamous organized crime groups originated in Italy during the 19th century. Today, the word is used to describe criminal groups from all over the world. In Russia and the other former Soviet states, organized criminal gangs are known as *mafiya*.

The Russian mafiya is not a single organization. It is made up of hundreds of small gangs known as *bratva* ("brotherhood"). Members of a particular *bratva* often have something in common: they may be from the same region or share a common ethnicity. These groups sometimes work together and sometimes fight for control of illegal rackets, such as territories where they control drug trafficking or prostitution.

Russian mafiya gangs originated in the gulag, a system of Soviet prisons and work camps for criminals and opponents of the Communist regime. An underground criminal society with its own rules of conduct, known as *Vorovskoy mir*, flourished in the gulags. Leading criminals, known as *vory v zakone* ("thieves in law"), became leaders of various prison groups.

In the mid-1950s, the gulag system was abolished and the Soviet government loosened some social and legal restrictions on its citizens. This led to an increase in criminal activity. Because of their experience, Russian mafiya groups had the organization to take full advantage of the new circumstances.

In the Soviet Union, the government controlled all businesses, and was supposed to provide all the necessities of life to the workers. In reality, however, food, essential items, and consumer goods were often rationed or unavailable. As a result, illegal "black markets" flourished in everything from clothes and groceries to alcohol and automobiles. The mafiya worked with corrupt Soviet government officials to steal items that could be resold on the black market. Both politicians and criminals grew rich from their collaboration.

During the mid-1980s, Soviet leader Mikhail Gorbachev introduced major economic reforms. *Perestroika*, or "restructuring," opened the Soviet economy, making private ownership of certain businesses legal. The changes gave people more freedom, easing the power of the state in everyday life. However, as in the past, when the Soviet government's tight grip loosened, criminal activity flourished.

After the dissolution of the Soviet Union in 1991, the economy of Russia and the other 13 former Soviet states experienced a drastic downturn. Corruption was already widespread in

When Vladimir Putin became president of Russia in 2000, he promised to crack down on criminal activity. However, during his more than 12 years in power the Russian mafiya has gained an extraordinary degree of influence and power in the country. In Russia, and in the other former Soviet republics, government corruption is widespread and criminal gangs operate with little fear of police interference.

Soviet surface-to-air missiles, such as this SA-6 system, give drug cartels an effective weapon to attack helicopters, which law enforcement agencies use to move troops quickly to attack cocaine and heroin laboratories in hard-to-reach jungle outposts.

government, the police force, and businesses. With unstable governments, the former Soviet republics were ripe for the picking. The Russian mafiya infiltrated the banking system, extorted money from businesses, and orchestrated credit card fraud. They also modernized, using new technology that allowed them to branch out and operate on an international scale.

Today the Russian mafiya operates in about 50 countries, including the United States. The Russians initially based their American criminal activities in the Brighton Beach and Sheepshead Bay sections of Brooklyn in New York City. Soon, the mafiya expanded into Miami and Puerto Rico.

Among the most lucrative activities of Russian mafiya groups are drug and weapons smuggling. Along with economic collapse, the demise of the Soviet

Union brought political strife to many of the former Soviet republics. Beginning in the early 1990s, the Russian mafiya took advantage of this instability by working with corrupt members of the Red Army to steal military supplies, which could then be sold to different factions in many countries around the world, particularly in Central Asia, Latin America, and Africa.

Russian mobsters also sold weapons and military supplies to drug cartels which they could use to smuggle shipments into the United States, and protect themselves from rivals or from government raids. By the late 1990s, Colombian drug cartels had purchased Soviet surface-to-air missiles, which could be used to shoot down government helicopters carrying police or soldiers who were raiding illicit drug labs in the Colombian jungle. The cartels had also purchased their own Soviet combat helicopters, which would give traffickers a more secure way to transport drugs. In one 1997 case, a Rusian mobster even offered to sell a Soviet submarine to a Colombian drug lord. The DEA arrested the gangster before the deal could be completed, however.

The arms sales led to closer ties between the mafiya and drug cartels. The mafiya could provide access to new drug markets in Russia as well as the other former Soviet republics. In some cases, the drug lords exchanged tons of

Colombian cocaine for Russian weapons.

A Russian mafiya gang called Solntsevskaya Bratva is believed to operate worldwide in narcotics and arms trafficking. Solntsevskaya Bratva is considered to be one of the most dangerous criminal organizations in the world. Its leader is Sergei "Mikhas" Mikhailov.

Criminal groups from the Chechnya region of Russia are also heavily involved in drug trafficking, thanks to this region's proximity to Afghanistan and Pakistan. Afghanistan is the world's foremost region for growing poppies, the juice of which can be processed into opium, morphine, and heroin. Poppies also grow well in Pakistan, and the country contains many illegal labs that can turn the plants into illegal narcotics. Hashish is another drug that is grown and processed in this region, and exported to Russia, as well as to countries in Central Asia and Europe, by Chechen gangsters. Political unrest, particularly in Afghanistan, has made it easier for mafiya smuggglers to operate. By the late 1990s the Russian mafiya had largely gained control of the heroin trade from the Sicilian mafia, which had previously controlled distribution of this drug into Europe and the United States. The largest Chechen group is called the Obshina.

The Pankisi Gorge region of the former Soviet republic of Georgia has emerged as another key location for drug smugglers. The gorge is located on the border of the Chechen region of Russia. Because of strained relations between Russia and Georgia, and a long-running Chechen rebellion against the Russian government, the gorge is very difficult to police. The mafiya has

In 1997 Russian mobster Ludwig "Tarzan" Fainberg attempted to sell a Soviet Tango-class patrol submarine to the Cali cartel. The sub, which is capable of operating underwater for up to a week, could have carried 40 tons of cocaine per trip from Colombia to the coast of California.

An Afghan farmer holds the fruit of an opium poppy. The juice of this plant is extracted from this bulb, and can be processed into opium, morphine, and heroin. All three are sold illegally; heroin is among the most popular of illicit drugs. Russian mafiya gangs have come to dominate the heroin trade in Europe, thanks in part to their proximity to the central Asian countries where the opium poppy grows well.

taken advantage of this chaos and used the gorge as a conduit to move drugs into Georgia and Russia.

In the United States, Russian mafiya groups had focused primarily on white collar crimes, like tax fraud or credit card scams, during the early 1990s. However, the American mafiya gangs soon became involved in drug trafficking. Working with Russian mafiya gangs, the American branch of the mafiya was able to supply drugs like heroin to the Italian-American mafia, which had previously imported the drug from the Sicilian mafia.

The Russian mafiya's involvement in the drug trade is not exclusively about making and distributing illegal substances. Russian mobsters have expertise in laundering money, and they offer this valuable service to drug cartels around the world. The Russian mafiya has set up financial operations in a number of Caribbean countries that have fairly lax banking regulations, such as Aruba, St. Vincent, and Antigua. In exchange for a share of the profits, the Russian mafiya launders money for drug cartels from Colombia, Mexico, Nigeria, and other countries. This makes cash from drug sales harder for anti-drug agents to trace.

In recent years the Russian mafiya has established alliances with various Mexican drug cartels and criminal gangs. Some Russian mafiya groups have started establishing businesses in Mexico, while also purchasing narcotics and smuggling them to Russia and the other former Soviet states.

Cash in the Closets
The Strange Case of Zhenli Ye Gon

On March 20, 2007, Mexican federal agents raided a large mansion in Mexico City's fashionable Lomas de Chapultepec district. The home was owned by Zhenli Ye Gon, a Chinese-born businessman who owned a pharmaceutical wholesale business, Unimed Pharm Chem México. The Mexican police were acting on a tip from the U.S. Drug Enforcement Agency, which suspected Ye Gon was using his company to smuggle pseudoephedrine, the main ingredient in crystal meth, from Mexico into the United States.

When federal police searched the mansion, they were surprised at what they found—cabinets, closets, and suitcases stuffed with cash. The currency weighed more than two tons, and included $205.6 million in American $100 bills, plus another $1.6 million in Mexican pesos and Hong Kong dollars.

Agents called it the largest drug-cash seizure in history. Weapons, vehicles, and drug-making equipment were also seized during the raid.

A few months later American police would arrest the home's owner, Zhenli Ye Gon, and accuse him of involvement in a major drug ring. But the case would not turn out to be so straightforward, taking many unexpected turns over the next few years.

Zhenli Ye Gon was born on January 31, 1963, in Shanghai, China. After being trained in pharmaceutical labs, he gained legal residence in Mexico in 1997, where he worked for two years at Laboratorios Silanes, a pharmaceutical company based in Mexico City. In 1999 he received government permission to start his own company, Unimed Pharm Chem de México.

In 2002, Ye Gon was officially granted Mexican citizenship. That same year

Pile of cash found at the home of Zhenli Ye Gon when the Mexican police raided in March 2007.

ries in Mexico—several of which were fronts for drug cartels that were producing crystal meth and smuggling it into the United States.

In 2005 it became illegal to import pseudoephedrine into Mexico, and Unimed's license expired on July 1 of that year. However, Ye Gon and some of his employees continued to secretly import pseudoephedrine, or the chemicals needed to make the substance, into Mexico during late 2005 and 2006. The company would purchase the chemicals in China and ship them secretly to Ye Gon's facility in Mexico.

the Mexican government awarded a license to Unimed, allowing the company to import thousands of metric tons of pseudoephedrine and ephedrine products into Mexico in order to make cold medicine. The chemicals were then resold to other laborato-

In 2006, Mexican drug agents discovered a ship from Hong Kong that was carrying more than 19 tons of a key chemical used to make pseudoephedrine.

American and Mexican drug agents believe Zhenli Ye Gon was working with the Sinaloa Cartel to produce crystal meth. However, the Mexican businessman has never been convicted of wrongdoing.

The ship arrived at the Mexican port of Lázaro Cárdenas with false paperwork. An investigation linked the chemicals to Unimed and Ye Gon. "There was evidently a falsification of documents that took place at some moment after the product left Chinese territory," explained Mexican Attorney General Eduardo Medina Mora.

This led Mexican and U.S. agents to investigate Ye Gon. As they uncovered evidence about the extent of his drug smuggling, a raid was ordered on his home. There, they found more than $207 million in cash, along with company and bank records that helped bring the scope of Ye Gon's operation into focus.

Ye Gon was not captured in the raid, and he soon entered the United States using a Chinese passport. In July 2007 the U.S. government indicted him, charging Ye Gon as part of a conspiracy to import crystal meth into the United States. He was arrested later that month while eating dinner in a Maryland restaurant.

Case File

Zhenli Ye Gon

Born: *January 31, 1963*

Known for: *Chinese-born Mexican citizen who operated a drug company. Alleged to have used his company to illegally procure key ingredients needed to produce crystal meth for the Sinaloa Cartel, and to have laundered millions in illegal funds*

Outcome: *Arrested 2007; currently in U.S. prison awaiting trial*

In federal custody, Ye Gon claimed that the huge amount of cash found in his home was not his profits from illegal drugs, as the government said. Instead, he claimed that representatives of the political party that ruled Mexico, the Partido Acción Nacional (PAN), had forced him to hide the cash in his home.

Ye Gon said that the funds were meant to be used secretly by the president of Mexico, Felipe

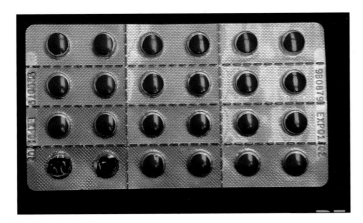

American laws make it very difficult for people to buy large quantities of medicines that contain pseudoephedrine. This has led to a major drop in the amount of methamphetamine made in the U.S.—which created a new opportunity for drug cartels that can produce crystal meth in Mexico.

In Las Vegas, Ye Gon reportedly bet up to $100,000 a hand on the card game baccarat. He did most of his gambling at the Venetian casino. This casino is controlled by Sheldon Adelson, who in 2012 was investigated for links to Chinese organized crime groups.

Calderón, who had won a disputed election in 2006. Ye Gon claimed that a politician named Javier Lozano Alarcón, who headed Calderón's election campaign, had ordered Ye Gon to hold the cash, threatening to have him killed if he refused. "I am an innocent victim and I was blackmailed to participate in these activities of the corrupt politics of Mexico," Ye Gon wrote in a letter. Calderón, Alarcón, and other Mexican officials dismissed his accusation as untrue.

Meanwhile, the DEA found that between 2004 and 2007, Ye Gon had gambled about $125 million in Las Vegas casinos. Casino gambling is a method some drug lords used to launder money at the time, although today there are rules and procedures that make this more difficult for criminals. The DEA alleged that Ye Gon would enter a casino and exchange his cash for gambling chips. After playing for a while, Ye Gon would turn in his chips, receiving a check from the casino. He could then put the check into his bank account and claim that he had won the money from gambling.

U.S. government prosecutors spent two years working on the case against Ye Gon. But in August 2009, the government dropped the case. They could not get witnesses to testify against the suspected drug lord, and it appeared some of their evidence would not be admitted in court.

Despite the case being dropped, Ye Gon has been living in an American prison since 2009. U.S. officials have been trying to send him to Mexico, where he could be tried in a Mexican court. However, through his lawyers Ye Gon has fought the extradition, claiming that he cannot get a fair trial in Mexico because of the political corruption. The strange saga of the businessman suspected to be a drug lord will probably not be resolved for several years.

Federal Drug Trafficking Penalties

Federal Trafficking Penalties for Schedules I, II, III, IV, and V (except Marijuana)				
Schedule	Substance/Quantity	Penalty	Substance/Quantity	Penalty
II	Cocaine 500-4999 grams mixture	**First Offense:** Not less than 5 yrs. and not more than 40 yrs. If death or serious bodily injury, not less than 20 yrs. or more than life. Fine of not more than $5 million if an individual, $25 million if not an individual. **Second Offense:** Not less than 10 yrs. and not more than life. If death or serious bodily injury, life imprisonment. Fine of not more than $8 million if an individual, $50 million if not an individual.	Cocaine 5 kilograms or more mixture	**First Offense:** Not less than 10 yrs. and not more than life. If death or serious bodily injury, not less than 20 yrs. or more than life. Fine of not more than $10 million if an individual, $50 million if not an individual. **Second Offense:** Not less than 20 yrs, and not more than life. If death or serious bodily injury, life imprisonment. Fine of not more than $20 million if an individual, $75 million if not an individual. **2 or More Prior Offenses:** Life imprisonment. Fine of not more than $20 million if an individual, $75 million if not an individual.
II	Cocaine Base 28-279 grams mixture		Cocaine Base 280 grams or more mixture	
IV	Fentanyl 40-399 grams mixture		Fentanyl 400 grams or more mixture	
I	Fentanyl Analogue 10-99 grams mixture		Fentanyl Analogue 100 grams or more mixture	
I	Heroin 100-999 grams mixture		Heroin 1 kilogram or more mixture	
I	LSD 1-9 grams mixture		LSD 10 grams or more mixture	
II	Methamphetamine 5-49 grams pure or 50-499 grams mixture		Methamphetamine 50 grams or more pure or 500 grams or more mixture	
II	PCP 10-99 grams pure or 100-999 grams mixture		PCP 100 grams or more pure or 1 kilogram or more mixture	

Substance/Quantity	Penalty
Any Amount Of Other Schedule I & II Substances Any Drug Product Containing Gamma Hydroxybutyric Acid Flunitrazepam (Schedule IV) 1 Gram	**First Offense:** Not more that 20 yrs. If death or serious bodily injury, not less than 20 yrs. or more than Life. Fine $1 million if an individual, $5 million if not an individual. **Second Offense:** Not more than 30 yrs. If death or serious bodily injury, life imprisonment. Fine $2 million if an individual, $10 million if not an individual.
Any Amount Of Other Schedule III Drugs	**First Offense:** Not more than 10 yrs. If death or serious bodily injury, not more that 15 yrs. Fine not more than $500,000 if an individual, $2.5 million if not an individual. **Second Offense:** Not more than 20 yrs. If death or serious injury, not more than 30 yrs. Fine not more than $1 million if an individual, $5 million if not an individual.
Any Amount Of All Other Schedule IV Drugs (other than one gram or more of Flunitrazepam)	**First Offense:** Not more than 5 yrs. Fine not more than $250,000 if an individual, $1 million if not an individual. **Second Offense:** Not more than 10 yrs. Fine not more than $500,000 if an individual, $2 million if other than an individual.
Any Amount Of All Schedule V Drugs	**First Offense:** Not more than 1 yr. Fine not more than $100,000 if an individual, $250,000 if not an individual. **Second Offense:** Not more than 4 yrs. Fine not more than $200,000 if an individual, $500,000 if not an individual.

Chapter

Notes

p. 9:   "[American politicians and law enforcement agencies] pretend . . ." Sari Horwitz, "U.S. Cities become Hubs for Mexican Drug Cartels' Distribution Networks," *Washington Post* (November 3, 2012). http://www.washingtonpost.com/world/national-security/us-cities-become-hubs-of-mexican-drug-cartels/2012/11/03/989e21e8-1e2b-11e2-9cd5-b55c38388962_story.html

p. 19:   "Many U.S.-based gangs . . ." Federal Bureau of Investigation, "2011 National Gang Threat Assessment." http://www.fbi.gov/stats-services/publications/2011-national-gang-threat-assessment

p. 21:   "He was a gangster . . ." Mark Bowden, *Killing Pablo: The Hunt for the World's Greatest Outlaw* (New York: Atlantic Monthly Press, 2001), p. 23.

p. 28:   "According to the philosophy . . ." William R. Long, "Unlike Their Medellín Brethren, They Shun Open Violence: The Cali Cartel: Colombia's Gentlemen Cocaine Traffickers," *Los Angeles Times* (August 17, 1989). http://articles.latimes.com/1989-08-17/news/mn-735_1_cali-cartel

p. 31:   "Easy boys. Don't kill me. . . ." Steven Ambrus and Kenneth Freed, "Reputed Leader of Cali Drug Cartel Captured," *Los Angeles Times* (June 10, 1995). http://articles.latimes.com/1995-06-10/news/mn-11704_1_cali-cartel

p. 33:   "These guilty pleas deal . . ." U.S. Department of Justice press release, "Cali Cartel Leaders Plead Guilty to Drug and Money Laundering Conspiracy Charges" (September 26, 2006). http://www.justice.gov/opa/pr/2006/September/06_crm_646.html

p. 55:   "Amado [Carrillo] is committed . . ." Markl Fineman, "U.S. Tags 'Lord of the Skies' as Mexico's Drug Kingpin,' *Los Angeles Times* (November 19, 1995). http://articles.latimes.com/1995-11-19/news/mn-4945_1_drug-cartels

p. 58:   "La Familia doesn't . . ." William Finnegan, "Silver or Lead," *The New Yorker* (May 31, 2010). http://www.newyorker.com/reporting/2010/05/31/100531fa_fact_finnegan#ixzz2JJEL7Hea

p. 63:   "Vengan por otro . . ." George W. Grayson, "La Familia Michoacána: A Deadly Mexican Cartel Revisited," Foreign Policy Research Institute (April 2009). http://www.fpri.org/enotes/200908.grayson.lafamiliamihoacana.html

p. 64:   "We have dealt . . ." U.S. Department of Justice press release, "More than 300 Alleged La Familia Cartel Members and Associates Arrested in Two-Day National Takedown," (October 2009). http://www.justice.gov/opa/pr/2009/October/09-ag-1135.html

p. 65:   "unusual and extraordinary threat . . ." U.S. Department of the Treasury, "An Overview of Sanctions Against Transnational Criminal Organizations."

http://www.treasury.gov/resource-center/sanctions/Programs/Documents/tco.txt

p. 66: "In [El Salvador], we were taught . . ." Mandalit del Barco, "The International Reach of the Mara Salvatrucha," NPR All Things Considered, March 17, 2005. http://www.npr.org/2005/03/17/4539688/the-international-reach-of-the-mara-salvatrucha

p. 69: "We want to prevent . . ." Matthew DeLuca, "Will Treasury's Crackdown on MS-13 Work?" *The Daily Beast*, October 17, 2012. http://www.thedailybeast.com/articles/2012/10/17/will-treasury-s-crackdown-on-ms-13-work.html

p. 71: "There's no doubt . . ." David Holthouse, "Leaders of Racist Prison Gang Aryan Brotherhood Face Federal Indictment," *Southern Poverty Law Center Intelligence Report*, Issue no. 119 (Fall 2005). http://www.splcenter.org/get-informed/intelligence-report/browse-all-issues/2005/fall/smashing-the-shamrock?page=0,1

p. 72: "If blacks attack whites . . ." David Holthouse, "Former 'Commissioner' John Greschner Discusses Life and Death in the Aryan Brotherhood," *Southern Poverty Law Center Intelligence Report*, Issue no. 148 (Winter 2012).

p. 81: "There was evidently a falsification . . ." Mark Sherman, "Alleged Drug Trafficker Indicted," USA Today (July 26, 2007). http://usatoday30.usatoday.com/news/topstories/2007-07-26-4178902933_x.htm

p. 82: "I am an innocent victim . . ." Hector Tobar and Carlos Martinez, "The $207-million Question in Mexico," *Los Angeles Times* (July 17, 2007). http://articles.latimes.com/2007/jul/17/world/fg-mexcash17

Glossary

cartel—a group of product producers who join together to control distribution and pricing of the product. Drug cartels are involved in the production, smuggling, and distribution of illegal drugs like cocaine, heroin, marijuana, and methamphetamines.

corruption—when a person who holds a government position or an elected office abuses the power of that position for personal gain. For example, a police officer who accepts a bribe in exchange for not reporting criminal activity.

decriminalize—to remove or reduce the criminal classification or status of; to repeal a strict ban on while keeping under some form of regulation.

de facto—in fact; in reality.

dissolution—the process of breaking something into smaller component parts or elements.

echelon—a level of command, organization, or rank.

extradition—the official process by which one country turns over custody of a person suspected or convicted of criminal activity to another country.

hashish—a drug made from the leaves and buds of the cannabis plant that have been processed to increase their potency, then compressed into a solid form. When smoked or ingested, hashish provides a more potent narcotic effect than marijuana.

informant—a person who provides secrets or important information about criminal activity to a police force or government agency.

logistics—the management of goods being shipped, such as illicit drugs, to ensure that they get from their point of origin to their destination safely.

lucrative—producing profit or wealth.

monolithic—something that is composed of a single unit and is characterized by a rigid, fixed uniformity.

mule—individual smugglers who attempt to carry drugs across the border, often hidden in their clothing or luggage or inside their bodies.

narco-state—a derogatory term for a country that is controlled and corrupted by drug dealers.

nexus—the place where things come together; the center of an organized group or network.

notorious—well-known or famous due to unfavorable or illegal activities.

OPEC—an acronym referring to the Organization of Petroleum Exporting Countries, an international cartel that attempts to influence the price of oil by controlling the amount produced by member states.

paramilitary—a force that is well armed and organized like a professional military, but is not part of a state's official armed forces.

patent medicines—medications sold without a prescription in the 1800s and early 1900s.

pseudoephedrine—a synthetic form of ephedrine, a stimulant that occurs naturally in certain plants. Pseudoephedrine is used as a decongestant in many legal over-the-counter medications, and is also required for the production of methamphetamine, which is illegal. Pseudoephedrine is mainly produced in China and India.

scuttle—to deliberately sink a ship by allowing water to flow into the hull.

traffic—to transport and trade certain goods, often ones that are not legal. Drug traffickers deliver and sell illegal drugs, for example, while human traffickers provide people for prostitution or forced labor.

Smugglers send the proceeds from their illegal drug sales south to the cartels in Mexico, often using creative methods to hide the cash. This drug money was found hidden inside a drum set.

Further Reading

Bowden, Mark. *Killing Pablo: The Hunt for the World's Greatest Outlaw*. New York: Atlantic Monthly Press, 2001.

Campos, Isaac. *Home Grown: Marijuana and the Origins of Mexico's War on Drugs*. Chapel Hill: University of North Carolina Press, 2012.

Dinges, John. *Our Man in Panama: How General Noriega Used the United States— and Made Millions in Drugs and Arms*. New York: Random House, 1990.

Escobar, Roberto, with David Fisher. *The Accountant's Story: Inside the Violent World of the Medillín Cartel*. New York: Grand Central Publishing, 2009.

Grillo, Ioan. *El Narco: Inside Mexico's Criminal Insurgency*. New York: Bloomsbury Press, 2011.

Harding, Luke. *Expelled: A Journalist's Descent into the Russian Mafia State*. New York: Palgrave Macmillan, 2012.

Kuhn, Cynthia, et al. *Buzzed: The Straight Facts about the Most Used and Abused Drugs from Alcohol to Ecstasy*. New York: W.W. Norton, 2008.

Longmire, Sylvia. *Cartel: The Coming Invasion of Mexico's Drug Wars*. Palgrave Macmillan, 2011.

Newton, Michael. *Criminal Investigations: Gangs and Gang Crime*. New York: Chelsea House Publishing, 2008.

Rempel, William C. *At the Devil's Table: The Untold Story of the Insider Who Brought Down the Cali Cartel*. New York: Random House, 2011.

Internet Resources

www.justice.gov/dea/index.shtml

The Drug Enforcement Administration is the government agency charged with investigating the illegal narcotics trade in the United States. The DEA, which is part of the U.S. Department of Justice, also helps local police departments track and arrest drug dealers.

www.pbs.org/wgbh/pages/frontline/shows/drugs

Companion website to the PBS Frontline documentary *Thirty Years of America's Drug War*.

www.monitoringthefuture.org

The University of Michigan's publishing an annual report on drug use by young people, *Monitoring the Future*, which can be accessed at this site.

www.whitehouse.gov/ondcp

The White House Office of National Drug Control Policy develops a national strategy to combat illegal drug use and serves as a liaison linking the different federal drug investigation and research agencies.

www.history.army.mil/brochures/Just%20Cause/JustCause.htm

This site, from the U.S. Army Center of Military History, offers a detailed account of the U.S. invasion of Panama, known as "Operation Just Cause."

www.fas.org/sgp/crs/row/RL34215.pdf

This site contains a report prepared for the U.S. Congress by an analyst in Latin American affairs. The report "provides an overview of: Mexican cartels and their operations, including the nature of cartel ties to gangs; Mexican cartel drug production in the United States; and the presence of Mexican cartel cells in the United States."

www.loc.gov/rr/frd/pdf-files/RussianOrgCrime.pdf
   This 2002 report from the U.S. Library of Congress provides an assessment of Russian organized crime groups, criminal elements in the Russian military, and groups involved in narcotics trafficking in Russia and Central Asia.

www.justice.gov/criminal/ocgs/gangs/prison.html
   This site from the U.S. Department of Justice provides information about several of the prominent prison gangs in the United States.

www.latimes.com/news/local/cartel/la-me-cartel-20110724,0,6282239.story
   "Unraveling Mexico's Sinaloa Drug Cartel" is a four-part report by the Los Angeles Times, published in 2011, that provides an overview of how the Mexican cartel smuggles drugs into the United States.

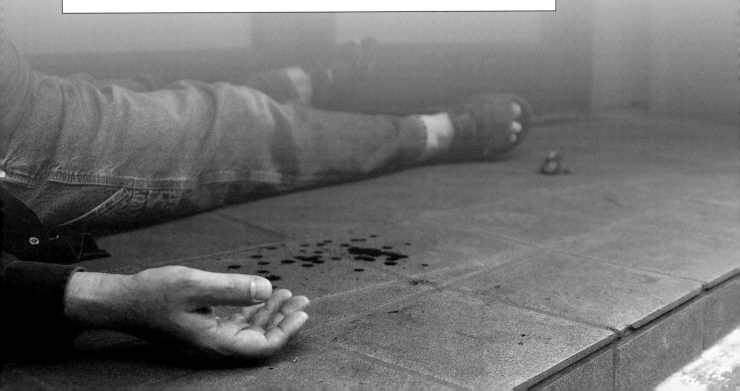

Publisher's Note: The Web sites listed on these pages were active at the time of publication. The publisher is not responsible for Web sites that have changed their address or discontinued operation since the date of publication.

Index

Numbers in **bold italics** refer to captions.

About the Authors

Carol Ellis has written several books for young people. Her subjects have included law in Ancient Greece, the Gilded Age, endangered species, martial arts, and women's rights. She lives in New York.

Robert Grayson is an award-winning former daily newspaper reporter. He is the author of numerous books for young adults, and has had articles published in many magazines.

Photo Credits: Drug Enforcement Administration: 2, 8, 11, 12, 13, 16, 18, 20, 29, 48, 49 (bottom), 60, 64, 69, 72, 80 (top), 81, 88; EFE: 30, 32, 55, 63, 80 (bottom); courtesy Federal Bureau of Investigation: 57; Federal Bureau of Prisons: 73; Getty Images: 56; AFP/Getty Images: 26; Gamma-Rapho via Getty Images: 24; OTTN Publishing: 44; used under license from Shutterstock, Inc.: 6, 22, 47, 51, 54, 61, 70, 77; Cafebeanz Company / Shutterstock.com: 82; ES James / Shutterstock.com: 66, 68; Meunierd / Shutterstock.com: 36; United Nations photo: 30, 33, 49 (top), 75, 78; U.S. Army photo: 9; U.S. Border Patrol: 15, 43; U.S. Coast Guard photo: 14, 59; U.S. Customs and Border Protection: 17; U.S. Department of Defense: 34, 38, 39, 40, 76; Wikimedia Commons: 25.

Cover Images: U.S. Customs and Border Protection (main); QiLux/Shutterstock.com (left inset); Drug Enforcement Administration (front insets, back).